Published October 2011
by Joy Publications
17 Farrant Way
Borehamwood Herts
WD6 4TE
berniewooder@hotmail.com

ISBN 978-0-9560751-1-6

Set in 11/14pt New Baskerville
Designed and typeset by Ed Fredenburgh
ed.fredenburgh@mac.com

Printed by Lightning Source
Milton Keynes MK11 3LW

Also by Bernie Wooder:
Movie Therapy: How it Changes Lives
Rideau Lakes Publishing 2008

NO ORDINARY LIFE

NO ORDINARY LIFE

Buddhism, psychotherapy,
and movies

Bernie Wooder UKCP

ABOUT THE AUTHOR

Bernie Wooder was born 6 August 1940 in London's East End. He is a fully trained and UKCP-accredited psychotherapist and counsellor with 20 years' experience and his own private practice. He is qualified in Core Process Psychotherapy and until 2004 had a practice in Harley Street.

A film buff from childhood, Bernie Wooder has pioneered the use of movies as an aspect of the therapeutic process for over 15 years. His commissioned work has included consultancy projects on movie therapy for MGM Studios and Warner Brothers, and presentations to student therapists at Guys Teaching Hospital in London and to media students at Leeds Trinity University.

As a member of the UK Council of Psychotherapists he contributes regularly to TV, radio and press and is currently conducting a series of lectures and workshops on movie therapy. He is the author of *Movie Therapy, How it Changes Lives,* published by Rideau Lakes in 2008.

Bernie lives with his wife Joy, son Jamie, daughter Claire, and granddaughter Amber in Borehamwood, Hertfordshire—appropriately enough on the doorstep of Elstree Film and Television Studios.

For my wife and family
who put up with me writing this book!

viii

CONTENTS

x

FOREWORD

A s the title indicates, no life is ordinary. Terms such as 'ordinary', 'normal', 'average' indicate abstractions, representatives that are torn from the living soil of events, gestures, responses. Each person's life is the flow of the unique specificity of each moment of his or her experience.

In these chapters Bernie shows his life unfolding in interaction with his lived environment. People, places, events both inform him and call him forth in the new forms of the successive phases of his existence.

The simplicity of the presentation allows the reader to encounter the intimate co-emergence of individual and context and through this each of us can perhaps see the revelation of our lives in a new light.

James Low
Consultant Psychotherapist, Guys Hospital, London

PREFACE

The word 'synchronicity' is going to force its way into anything I attempt to write about Bernie, so I take synchronicity as the place to begin.

"When the disciple is ready, the guru will appear," says an old Indian proverb. Doubtless, Bernie would reject the term 'guru' as applied to himself, but the proverb communicates exactly my sense of the timeliness of his appearances in my own life.

When I first met Bernie, at a conference on film and personal development, his directness and simplicity of approach to a subject matter I always tend to overcomplicate took me by surprise. He is a man who communicates at a very straightforwardly personal level, gentle, receptive—and so strongly grounded that you feel it wouldn't be possible to push him over. It is as if his energy flows from deep down, almost from the earth beneath his feet. As someone who is always inclined to fly off into airy nothings, I found that Bernie's presence as much as what he said was a lesson in being there, in settling into oneself. It came as a timely gift, at a moment when I needed the strength to settle into some difficult recognitions of my own, this willingness to listen and ability to hear what is really being said, even when one doesn't recognise it oneself.

On more than one occasion since that first meeting, I've benefited from Bernie's extraordinary sixth sense of when it might be wise to pick up the phone. How does he do it? Search me! But he generally manages to choose a moment when his calm conversation is exactly the tonic needed to restore a lost perspective or open up a new vista on something that appears problematic.

Perhaps most importantly, he has the great gift of being completely unselfish in his dealings with others. He demonstrates the skill of setting others free, not binding to himself those with whom he spends his time.

Why haven't I mentioned film? Perhaps because I'm never really conscious of Bernie 'using' film as a technique in his dealings with me. Curious, really, but perhaps rightly so. The best special effects don't draw attention to themselves, they serve the narrative or character development of the story in which they feature.

Similarly, Bernie moves easily from personal experience to spiritual insight, through a Hollywood moment or two, and back to something that happened in the family. He hasn't said this to me, but I suspect that he would suggest the way he reflects with his clients and others on the role film plays in our lives is a paradigm for all sensitive reflection on experience. Perhaps, like dreams, film is a privileged ideogram of the soul, but my sense is that for Bernie it is the soul that matters, not the film.

Father Mark Barratt
WORTH ABBEY BENEDICTINE MONASTERY

INTRODUCTION

There are many reasons why I decided to write this book. It somehow seemed important to leave some record of the events and people who helped to shape my professional and spiritual development.

I trained at the Karuna Institute in Devon, which brought together western developmental psychology, Buddhist psychology and eastern meditation and awareness practices.

I hope the book may help people in their personal and professional lives, make some of them smile, be inspirational to others. It feels good for me to be able to express various moments of my life in a way that is the very opposite of listening and taking things in as a therapist.

I have been able to bring my love of films into my life as a therapist by pioneering and developing 'movie therapy' as a force for healing. I have therefore included in the book some case studies of my work with clients involving the use of film to show how this process works—what it is and what it is not.

I have also described my journey through cancer.

The book is not in strict chronological order and the experiences it covers, I now realise, represent only a small part of my life. Yet writing the book has given me a sense of my life as a journey and a stronger sense of continuity of being.

Note: All my clients who kindly agreed to be featured in this book chose their own 'cover names' so that their confidentiality was protected.

2

1 THE MAGIC KITCHEN

Our kitchen was filled with excitement once again as the latest film was discussed and re-enacted. I was standing there wide-eyed and totally fascinated as mum's friend Patsy Tricky captured the exact look, the exact mood.

This time she was acting out the film *Johnny Belinda*. The film's heroine, played by the actress Jane Wyman, was a mute girl whose every emotion had to be conveyed by the eyes. Patsy would do her bit brilliantly while my mum and I watched in rapt attention. Then my mum would say "And what about this bit?" becoming Johnny Belinda before our eyes. It was an amazing performance, as she looked absolutely nothing like Jane Wyman, but resembled if anything a cross between Maureen O'Hara and Angie Dickinson.

Mum and Patsy brought the cinema even more alive for me. They were wonderful storytellers and actresses with real talent. The war stripped life down to what was truly important: the essentials such as love, compassion and romance. These two women captured and gave expression to the wonder of love, the mystique of romance and the depths of despair or compassion.

These were moments of emotional truth expressed in our magic kitchen because my mum and her friend never knew if they would survive to live them. Talking about the latest film from beginning to end, they could make you cry and they would cry themselves, doing those scenes back and forth. They criticised those actresses and actors they didn't like with all the cattiness and humour that women love.

In later years my mum would give us terrific impressions of Maureen O'Hara, Susan Hayward, Peter Sallis, Dame Edna Everage, Alastair Sim and Lana Turner, to name but a few. First she did the look, with her sparkling blue eyes; next the way of talking, and then the whole body language would follow effortlessly. Her memory for whole tracts of dialogue was amazing. She had a great personality, full of fun. I loved to make her laugh because then I also laughed in the pure enjoyment of her laughter. It made me feel so good inside because the fun would build up more and more until you could not get enough of it. When she died part of my world stopped and went silent for ever.

No words can express how grateful I am to my mum for my incredibly rich early years—for her loving warmth and kindness. When you looked at her you could instantly see the intelligence and beauty shining from her face. She was a true fiery Leo with her laughing eyes and perceptive, hilarious one-liners. Being exposed to the dramatic and comedic talent of my mum and Patsy Tricky so early in my life and for so long left a lasting impression on me.

2 WAR BABY

When I was born in 1940 at London's University College Hospital every day was like New York on 9/11. From September of that year I was greeted by 51 days of consecutive bombing as the German Luftwaffe carpet bombed London in an attempt to hit the docks and to demoralise the British people.

Memories from the first six years of my life were imprinted on my young mind: black and red skies as far as you could see, the terrible sounds of the sirens, the air raid warnings and my parents' faces frozen in sheer panic.

I remember the conflict between them, my mum saying, "We're going to the shelter," but my dad saying, "No Mary, we'll be safer here." They had just a few minutes to make life or death decisions for all of us, yet they were so young. There was one incident that was quite humorous: I remember my mum and dad, Patsy Tricky and Aunt Agg, running in panic to the shelter as the air raid had started, with Aunt Agg repeatedly shouting "Those bastards will be the death of me!"—completely missing the point that that was their sole intention.

When we went to the shelter we would be huddled together, some people chatting in corners, babies and small children, some crying softly, some screaming. People would be helping one another, their kindness as evident as the shock and psychosis. In the tube the struggle was finding a place on the platforms to sleep. Someone would call, "There's space over here, darling." Aunt Agg would still be muttering, "Those bastards will be the death of me."

Another frightening incident: my mum and Patsy Tricky, out after the air raid warning had gone and running to get home, saw not far away chips of brick and concrete flying out of the walls. They looked up and realised they were being machine gunned by a German bomber. In that moment they just hugged one another instinctively and, to their surprise, started laughing uncontrollably together—obviously in hysteria and shock. I heard them go through this incident many times as they came to terms with their brush with death.

Sometimes we would go and listen to the band in Wilmington Square, which was built around gardens with a bandstand in the centre. When I was only three and a half my mum would say to me, "Bernard, you are going to sing to the people in the gardens." Percy Packard used to come with his band as part of a government effort to keep up morale. I once sang into a huge microphone standing on a chair and was nicknamed Sinatra Crosby. From then on I vividly remember my mum teaching me a new song for every time Percy Packard came.

My earliest memory is of being in my mum's arms looking up at the red and black night sky, acrid smoke filling the air. The red colour was coming from the numerous fires in a city aflame with incendiary bombs and doodlebugs—those unmanned planes with their familiar drone, followed by the eerie silence and then huge explosions, that paralysed everyone with fear. Sometimes I can't believe we lived through all of that.

3 TADWORTH

As I was walking along Exmouth Market one day my leg kept hurting.

"Mum," I asked, "could you carry me?"

"No Bernard, you're a big boy now."

"But Mum," I whined, "it really hurts."

"OK boy," she said softly and picked me up. She saw that I was indeed in pain and decided to make a medical appointment for me.

We arrived at Great Ormond Street Hospital and after giving me a thorough examination, the doctor said, with the coldly superior attitude of the time, "Mother, the boy will have to go into hospital." Mum looked ashen.

"What is it Doctor?" The doctor replied, "I suspect polio." My mum's shock was palpable, as she knew how deadly polio and TB were at that time.

"Can you help him?" she asked in a whisper, tears welling up.

"It's too early to say for sure," replied the doctor in the same emotionless tone. "He'll have to wear an iron."

"You mean he'll be a cripple?"

"Possibly," the doctor answered.

I was caught up in the maelstrom of my mum's suffering. How could I make her feel better? Then came the final *coup de grâce* from Dr Death—as I now think of him.

"He'll have to go into our hospital in Tadworth in Surrey."

My mum gasped, "But that's miles away."

"Yes, but it's best for the boy. I'll write soon when I have it all arranged."

My mum was in a dream, so sad, her bouncy walk now heavy. Then with a supreme effort of will she smiled at me and gave me the most wonderful hug I have ever experienced.

"It'll be alright, Bern. Don't worry, mummy will talk to daddy and find a way to visit." Her tears fell on my ear. Once again I was overwhelmed. I felt my lovely mum, so full of life, trembling with the shock, and I was powerless to help her.

Soon I was in hospital in Tadworth—an experience I remember mainly with dread, loneliness and despair. I had been diagnosed as having Perthes' Disease, a rare condition very similar in its symptoms to polio. I found myself confined to a cot for months on end with my leg in traction. This terrible period was to shape the rest of my life. My mum and dad could only visit once a month because of the long, expensive journey from our home in Clerkenwell. It was 1944 and I was four years old.

One day which began as drearily as the rest, I had what on reflection I can only see as an out of body experience. I was feeling the familiar dread when suddenly everything went quiet and calm in me. I was looking down from the ceiling, seeing myself in a small cot in a room with sparse furniture and pale green walls. I can feel its bareness still.

After quite a while I was suddenly back in my body and rested and immediately fell into a deep sleep. Was this the beginning of my spiritual life? Was this the forerunner to the witness in me that was to develop over the years and culminate in Buddhism? My mum told me I often said I wanted to be a priest when I grew up.

Because I was on a children's ward my sleep most nights was disturbed by little ones crying, and by frightening shadows on the walls created by the tall hats of the nurses. I was there so long that the nurses would use me as an example of bravery to the new children, who were understandably frightened and upset when they came in.

"Look at Bernard," they would say, "he's been here for two months." I would look suitably brave and from here I began to find my role.

Over time I made friends with the children in the beds either side of me but when they went home it was torture. Why not me? When I asked this or became upset I was given a sweet, cake or an extra pudding. This marked the beginning of my comfort eating and subsequent weight problem.

What I remember most was the lack of physical touch— no hugs. I missed terribly all the nurture and comfort from my mum, and the endless days waiting for my parents' monthly visit seemed intolerable. It was so painful I had to let die all hope and anticipation of their visits, because when the visits ended the emotional cost was greater than the benefit. The hurt, the despair and the overwhelming pain of this experience has shaped my life, given me an empathy for suffering that's in my bones, and made me who I am.

One image still comes to mind because, I now realise, it mirrored my inner feelings of loneliness. It was of the cold rain dripping on a rusty iron gate on yet another grey day.

After I had been bedridden for a year the time came for me to get out of bed. Two nurses helped me as, to my surprise, I couldn't walk at first. The pain in my hip had gone and no iron was needed for my leg. I started off by crawling, heckled by the cruel shouts of other children, before gradually beginning to walk again. I was by now five years old.

4 GROWING UP IN THE EAST END

I am often asked how I became a psychotherapist and when my love of films started. I developed my fondness for films from a very early age, when we were living in Clerkenwell. It was the 1940s and we were at war. My dad had gone to serve in the army leaving behind my mum, aged 19 and with me, a young baby. She was terrified of the daily bombings. To deal with the fear she would often take me to the pictures so she could escape the terror and constant worry about whether she and her baby would survive and whether she would see her husband again.

The Rio cinema was just a stone's throw from where we lived, so almost every time the programme changed my mother and I would be there. I was a very curious child and would ask her to explain to me the sometimes complicated and sophisticated love stories. It's not surprising that I became a psychotherapist. By the time I was six I was 'Barry Norman'.

Also I had developed an understanding of relationships and emotional issues way beyond my years and with the absence of my father I became my mum's confidant. This was to make my relationship with my father problematic in later years, as I understood my mum better than he did and he became very difficult.

My dad was very volatile and didn't suffer fools gladly. One funny incident I remember was the time he took me to have a suit made. On inspecting the finished suit he found a worn part in the material for the trousers so he asked the tailor to make them again. When they were ready for collection my dad scrutinised them.

"We agreed a new pair," he exploded. "These have been invisibly mended." Before I knew it he had the trousers round the tailor's neck, throttling him.

"You don't take me on," he said.

Another incident showed how fiercely protective my father was of his family. At that time after the war there were lots of bombed ruins where the kids would play. One day when I was playing with friends in the ruins and we had made a fire, some older youths came along and thought it was funny to hold me by the hair so my face was over the fire. I was coughing and spluttering from the smoke, and obviously very frightened.

Someone must have told my dad because he came charging across the ruins, waving a fireman's axe and shouting "Do you think this is funny?" I've never seen people run as fast as those two boys escaping with my dad in hot pursuit. I was so glad he didn't catch them. He was enraged, but afterwards showed great gentleness when he took me upstairs and washed my smoke-blackened face.

5 EPILEPSY

One night when I was 12 years old I was drifting off to sleep when I started to experience a tickly feeling and a twitching on the right side of my upper lip. It became stronger and stronger until the whole right side of my face began to twitch uncontrollably. My reaction was one of sheer terror. What was happening to me? Was I going to die? Then I lost consciousness.

I came round feeling very weak and nauseous. So began a period of epilepsy that was to last until I was 21. The pattern it took was an attack when I was falling asleep or just waking. In fact there were times when I had two attacks a day, one on waking up and one on going to sleep. The sense of weakness and nausea always followed, and my fear of sleeping and waking increased.

My mum and dad were very upset and felt totally helpless. My dad fixed up a little bell on my bedroom wall because, once an attack had started, I was unable to call loud enough to be heard. Even with the bell I was sometimes unable to raise the alarm before losing control of my body and becoming unconscious.

After numerous tests I was diagnosed as suffering from *petit mal* epilepsy. My mum was advised that at the onset of an attack, a spoon with a bandage wrapped around its end should be placed in my mouth to prevent me biting my tongue. I remember my parents being very relieved that it was not *grand mal* epilepsy, a more serious long term condition. Thankfully I seldom had an attack in the daytime, but my nausea and weakness could last for at least a couple of hours.

I was prescribed phenobarbitone, which controlled my attacks but unfortunately slowed down my mental processes. I felt as if I was trying to think with my brain full of treacle. It was a huge effort and very frustrating, made worse by the sheer ignorance of teachers at school.

One day in a maths lesson a particularly unpleasant teacher asked me to come up to the front of the class to solve a maths problem he had written on the blackboard. Of course I couldn't do it. I felt lost, in a daze.

"Come on Wooder, think, if that's possible," he said. I struggled, wanting at that moment to kill him. Then I just gave up. He continued to treat me like a cretin, to the great amusement of the class, wanting to inflict maximum humiliation. He sneered sadistically as he talked to me, his face full of hate.

Suddenly, in a shift of consciousness similar to the out of body experience I'd once had in hospital, I 'witnessed' the whole thing. I had a comfortable, calm clarity and just felt terrific. Within a few minutes the teacher was looking disconcerted.

"OK, Wooder, sit down," he said quietly. I don't know what took place but something happened in him as well.

I returned to my seat indifferent to the class, gazing out of the window in total calm at the pigeons on the roof. Out in the playground there was the familiar smell from the meat factory next door. Not long after this the bell went for the lunch break. As we all filed out I looked the teacher straight in the eye conveying all my rage and venom. He got the full force of it, even looking a little scared. One great value of anger is that it takes away fear. At such moments it is possible to understand murder in some situations.

Regarding the witness experience with the teacher, the question comes to me as I write: could I have been dissociating? I don't think so—the calmness and clarity was the same state as the witness in Vipassana meditation.

6 MEMORABLE CHARACTERS

WEST END ENCOUNTERS

When I first left school I got a job on the *Star* newspaper, delivering in London's West End. At seventeen I was distributing the original *Star* newspaper, one of the three big national papers of the time. I looked after deliveries in Piccadilly and the West End, handling those newspapers that could not be transported by van because it was such a congested area.

The procedure was that at 9am each morning we would fill up the van with papers at the depot in Stamford Street and drive to Piccadilly tube where they would be unloaded onto the pavement outside. I was responsible for seeing that the three boys working with me delivered the papers to all parts of the West End, on foot via the underground passageways in order to beat the traffic. While they were doing that I would catch another van and deliver to all the hotels and gentlemen's clubs around Park Lane.

MEMORABLE CHARACTERS

I came across many colourful characters and incidents during my time in the West End. One day I was counting the papers as usual in front of Piccadilly tube when a gruff voice from behind me asked, "Your name Wooder?" I turned round to see a big man with a scar down his left cheek dressed as if he had stepped out of a 1940s black and white gangster film. I replied warily that I was, whereupon he shook my hand with a vice-like grip and introduced himself.

"My name's Appy Sandwich. I knew your father—he was a good 'un."

I was transfixed. He was intimidating and friendly at the same time. He said, "I think I can put some business your way." I wondered nervously what kind of business he had in mind.

He explained that every day there would be Americans around, usually from Manston air base. They would have spent up in the Soho clip joints and would need money to get back to their base. They would usually have something to sell—watches, their Strategic Air Command rings, soriety rings or cameras.

"When you see them," said Appy, "just ask them if they want to sell anything and if they do, come and tell me."

The idea was that he would be waiting in a nearby coffee bar and if he did a deal I would get a share of the proceeds. I was surprised to find I earned more with Appy than I did on the *Star*.

As I got to know him better I had to ask him why he called himself Appy Sandwich. He explained, "As your Dad will tell you, son, we were all very poor years ago. I was always big and strong, so if anyone wanted anything done like clearing bricks or rubbish—anything manual—I would do it. And because they knew I loved my food I would get paid with jam sandwiches. As I sat eating them on my doorstep people would say, 'He's 'appy.' That's how I came to be known as Appy Sandwich."

Outside the London Pavilion was a paper seller. I was told to take my papers to 'Knobby over there'. When I approached him he turned round and I was shocked to see he had no face, just two holes where his nose should have been and nothing but a thin synthetic covering of his skin. He had been blown up in the war and I was so impressed by the way he was stoically carrying on with his life, even more so when the cold weather came because it was painful for him and he had to cover up quite a bit.

One Saturday evening I was delivering papers, hurrying down a narrow shopping street between Brewer Street and Berwick Market. In front of me at the end of the lane I saw two men beating up a third man. Suddenly one got hold of his arms, the other grabbed his legs and they threw him through a shop window. As I came nearer the man was thrown straight back through the window by the people inside and landed thump on his back on the pavement.

A new paper seller took over a pitch outside Monaco's restaurant in Shaftesbury Avenue and when I gave him his papers he thanked me in the deepest, poshest of voices. He turned out to be a down-on-his-luck opera singer of about 65. He always wore an old black Crombie overcoat with a carnation in his lapel and a black felt trilby hat that had seen better days. He looked as if he had stepped out of another time.

Some years later I had a job delivering newspapers in London's East End, where the infamous Jack the Ripper had terrified Victorian London in the streets surrounding Spitalfields.

One bitterly cold winter morning at 4am I was driving up to a shop to make a delivery. Standing there on the pavement was a young woman aged about 32 and wearing a very flimsy dress. As I pulled up she glanced at me like a frightened rabbit. The wind was particularly biting on the pavement where she was standing, and she shivered with cold and fear when I walked up to her.

"Can I help, love? What's happened?" I assured her everything was alright.

"You must be freezing," I said gently. She smiled faintly and murmured, "Yes, I just had to get away. I couldn't stand being hit any more." I then asked if she would like a lift to the nearest police station. She backed away at this and I had to be very cautious, unsure of how she perceived my offer of help at that moment. It was important to reassure her that I was not a threat.

"Look, you must go and stand in that phone box across the road where you'll at least be warmer and protected from the wind and rain." She went into the phone box dutifully, like a little girl. I felt in my pocket for some money for her, finding that I only had a ten pound note.

"There's a little cafe that opens shortly down here," I said, pointing to the turning. "Take this and go and have a cup of tea and something to eat."

At this she let out a terrified scream which frightened the living daylights out of me. She sobbed and sobbed, gently taking the money as she looked at me in puzzled disbelief. I got the feeling that it had been a very long time since she had experienced any kindness.

Then I suddenly realised the time. The newsagents were waiting for their papers so that the paper boys could deliver them on their bikes. I waved as I drove away, still in shock from that scream and those sobs. It was one of those moments I will never forget. I often wonder what happened to her and hope she found a better life.

FRIENDS ON FLEET STREET

Some time later I had left the *Star* and was working in Fleet Street at the *Daily Mail.* Fleet Street, then the home of all the national newspapers, was a most exciting place. It was the hub of world news and the characters there were interesting, streetwise Cockneys, full of fun and wonderfully eccentric. There were those dressed in ordinary work clothes—jeans and windcheaters—while others wore really smart tailored suits, exuding confidence. The cool ones could go from Fleet Street to any West End club and feel absolutely at home.

Some of my workmates were Dickensian-looking characters: some had disabilities, some had great voices, some were huge men but gentle giants, and some were bullies. Nearly all loved a drink.

One night I was working at the *Daily Mail* alongside Sid the Glove, parcelling up the newspapers as they came off the printing presses. Sid had dermatitis on his left hand and wore a single glove to hide it, hence he became known as Sid the Glove. It was 2.30am and about 500 of us were tying up the bundles when suddenly we heard the sound of bagpipes.

"Bagpipes?" muttered Sid, looking at me in bewilderment. "Bagpipes in Fleet Street?" We looked across the warehouse to see a man in full Scottish regalia marching vigorously. He was one of two eccentric brothers who drove the delivery vans.

This was as serious as the battle of Bannockburn to him. Laughter ensued and gradually a conga line formed behind him. Up and down we marched, our piper now inspired. (I'm sure he fancied himself as William Wallace in the film *Braveheart*.)

We were roaring with laughter as this spontaneous party erupted. One drunken man was now tap dancing, playing a mouth-organ out of tune and beaming a toothless smile at us all. When asked where his teeth were he replied, "I took them out, it helps me play better." Sid said, "Put 'em back in, you're off key!" More roars of laughter. The mouth-organ player took it all in good part and flashed us another huge smile.

"Blimey, he could eat a banana sideways!" a voice shouted above the chaos.

The conga line was now getting longer, hip flasks were out and the whisky and rum were flowing. To be fair, Fleet Street had always been well lubricated, but on this occasion the piper inspired the drinking.

Men were now doing their version of the Scottish reel, some with their trouser legs rolled up and displaying a variety of knobbly knees. One man had numerous pronounced varicose veins.

"Look at them," said Sid the Glove, "like Clapham Junction."

"Find your other glove," retorted the man. Sid laughed. He had beaten Michael Jackson by 40 years.

A circle had formed around the now out-of-breath mouth-organ player and the party's anthem became *Donald where's your troosers?* All those who knew the words were singing *Let the wind blow high, let the wind blow low*. Then the chorus thundered *Donald where's your troosers?* A spoon player had appeared to shouts of "Go on my son." Amazingly none of this hilarity interfered with the paper hitting the streets on time.

My friends in Fleet Street were intelligent and well-read. Many had other jobs as antique dealers, film extras, cab drivers, market stall holders, shopkeepers or professional gamblers. Not a few operated on both sides of the law. They were warm and generous, always ready to donate to a worthy cause such as the nurses' strike. In the miners' strike they sent lorry loads of food and toys for Christmas to the mining communities, and even stopped one issue of the *Sun* which was critical of the miners until management agreed to a right of reply. Above all, these were men who really knew how to enjoy life—seize the moment.

HERMAN DOLD

Sid the Glove and I became good friends. He invited my girlfriend and me to tour with him and his wife through France, Germany and Austria. Driving through the Black Forest, we stopped overnight at a beautiful inn on the banks of a lovely river. The proprietor was an older man called Herman Dold, who was conscious of us being English. As we drank schnapps, he joined us and apologised for the war, telling us he had been a Luftwaffe pilot who had been shot down and wounded. Eventually Sid, his wife, myself and my girlfriend were pretty far gone. Sid told me I ended up having a dance with Herman, and laughed as he reminded me that while I was dancing, I'd told him, "Sid, you'd never believe he got it in the leg!"

TOUGH JOB

It's funny when you look back over your life, reviewing all that you've done, some of the jobs. I remember a job I had with a bottling company. It consisted of emptying the wine cellars of the empty champagne bottles from the many gentlemen's clubs in Pall Mall, around the City and in Fleet Street. In those days, the cellars had their opening on the pavement outside a given bar. This meant when I had to carry champagne cases, for example, I had to climb a vertical steel ladder attached to the wall, with the hundredweight of empty bottles on my back, secured only with one hand whilst using the other to hold on to each rung as I climbed up the ladder to the pavement.

Champagne bottles are particularly heavy because, for one, they were particularly bulky bottles, and two, the corks were topped with lead. It was hard work. I soon became very fit, although I was always physically strong. I loved it and I could let my mind think, observe, go anywhere.

The first few days of this job were the toughest. I was sent with a driver to the huge railway yards at the top of Archway hill. There were miles of train tracks, with trains stationary along them. We had to find the carriages which were packed with new, clean, empty bottles.

It was snowing on and off, and the wind in those open yards was bitingly cold. The carriages had a huge steel lever to open them, but we found them frozen solid with ice. The driver, an old timer called Tom, said "Fuck it. Bernie, break that old palette up in the back, and bring me a couple of pieces a foot long." With that he set fire to them and we held them under the steel levers to melt the ice.

As I looked around this barren, snow covered siding, I thought, I am in Russia. The ice on the levers finally melted, though it took longer than I thought it would. When we pushed the carriage door open, we found roughwood cases stacked to the ceiling and full of bottles.

We started to unload them; it was back breaking work but it warmed me up. When the lorry was full, we delivered them to wine distilleries.

This took us all of three days. By the middle of the second day, the creases in my fingers started bleeding—made worse by the cold. I told to Tom, who just smiled and said, "Piss on them, they'll be fine." I was shocked.

"Do you mean that?"

"Yes, of course," he said, "there's acid in your piss: that'll heal them."

Tom rolled another cigarette, while I went to piss on my hands. I repeated this the next day, and amazingly it worked: but though the cuts dried up, the cuts in the creases remained open.

The yard manager at the depot was known as Mad Ernie. He was an incredibly tough, wiry little man, with thin lips and not an ounce of fat on him. He was dynamic, walking relentlessly up and down the yard, barking orders at people.

"Take that lorry there, get that wheel fixed before you go out."

We came back from delivering one day, to be told by one of the other drivers that Mad Ernie has broken his leg. It was a weekend and we went home. When we came back Monday, we were amazed to see Mad Ernie with his leg in plaster, tied to a Samson. A Samson for those, who don't know, was a small trolley, about two foot wide and three foot long. You could tip heavy cases on to it and just push them. Ernie had tied his broken leg to the Samson and was going up and down the yard. It was obviously slower, but clearly that broken leg wasn't going to get in Ernie's way. I don't think it ever occurred to Ernie to have time off.

7 WAPPING

I was working in the print at the time of the 1986 Wapping dispute. That was when media magnate Rupert Murdoch tried to break the print and journalists' unions by moving production of the *Times, Sunday Times, Sun* and *News of the World* to a plant in Wapping, east London. He wanted us to accept new technology and harsh anti-union working conditions; when we refused and went on strike he sacked thousands of us and hired other workers. We were forced to picket the Wapping plant to try to stop the papers being distributed.

The atmosphere on the picket line at Wapping in the beginning was a mixture of anger and anxiety. In the early stages of the picketing many families took part which introduced a feeling of community and much humour. Sadly the whole atmosphere changed and became menacing. The police were hard faced, even hate-filled in many cases, and the pickets responded in kind. The mutual hate seemed to be reinforced by the bitterly cold January winds sweeping up the Thames.

Wapping became a war zone as lines of mounted police with drawn batons and lines of pickets confronted each other. More and more people joined us, all of them incredibly determined. Their solidarity and courage, their protectiveness and care for one another were inspiring to me.

In one incident during a mounted police charge I got smashed against a barrier by a police horse. I was on the floor, winded, and couldn't talk or breathe for a moment which seemed like forever. My friends and other pickets rushed to my assistance and I heard one shouting to another to get me a tea with an urgency that was moving.

There was a constant hubbub as we waited for Murdoch's huge lorries to drive out with newspapers for that night's delivery. When the first lorry came out, a deafening roar of anger went up and the mood became ugly as enraged pickets surged forward to break through the police lines.

Sometimes when this happened riot police would appear in their black uniforms, helmets and protective visors. They banged their shields, hitting out right, left and centre with their batons at the heads of people who fell, ran and fought bravely. I did not see us as thugs but as warriors protecting our families. What angered me was that Murdoch, who had the power to mobilise this state machine against us, was not even in the country.

One night the familiar sound of people chatting and laughing turned to excitement as we heard the approach of 10,000 marching print workers. Police horses moved nervously, the tension mounted, then suddenly the marchers appeared and a huge roar went up from us all. As the marchers got closer the police moved into position, brandishing their batons and riot shields.

Someone threw a smoke bomb and red smoke drifted everywhere. The marchers broke through the police line and all hell let loose, with flying planks of wood being torn off fences and thrown at baton-wielding police moving forward on foot.

Now a signal came for the mounted police to charge. In the midst of this frightening chaos I worried about the horses as I don't think anyone wanted them to be hurt. The injured were taken for medical treatment and tea to the bus and caravan we had organised for this purpose.

As some people went home, having done their picketing shift, many others arrived and there was a mood of round the clock solidarity. The talk among the pickets was of how to deal with the power of the horses without hurting them. One old timer and army veteran who had spent much time in Africa suggested "What we need is some lions' piss—the horses will stop in their tracks and bolt." We were momentarily stunned into silence till someone asked jokingly "Where are we going to get lions' piss, London Zoo?" It was duly agreed that a couple of us would check this out.

There were often speakers who addressed the crowd of pickets. One night while Tony Benn MP was speaking from a quickly assembled platform, the lorries carrying papers suddenly started flying through the gates of the Wapping plant and the usual roar went up.

This time, for some tactical reason, the police riot squad approach was very different. Banging their shields and shouting they attacked the crowd listening to Tony Benn, hitting everyone indiscriminately. Tony Benn appealed to them to stop but the police totally ignored him. They had reached a state known psychologically as 'red mist' where they had lost control of themselves as a unit in the chaos of the crowd. People were crushed against the platform which now started to tip with Tony Benn on it, and he made a speedy exit to safety.

As I was going home I saw a shocking incident that has stayed with me to this day. A family was also leaving and when the 60 year-old mother threw away the residue of her cup of soup it was unfortunately caught by the wind and blown on to a nearby police inspector's shoulder. Furious, he ordered his officers to get hold of the woman. They proceeded to tip her upside down with one holding each of her legs. It was a lesson in public humiliation. Her family screamed and cried for her to be put down while the son, trying to protect his mum, was being held back by his sisters.

To be at Wapping was to experience the brutality of state power and the limitations of democracy. It was certainly history in the making.

I later talked to Tony Benn, who helped us by submitting an Early Day Motion about police violence at Wapping to the House of Commons. The following extracts are taken from his report:

> *"...From about 9.30 until I left at 12.30 there were just continual police charges on the crowd—mounted police moving at speed in all directions, waving their truncheons and shields.*
>
> *...I went over to the first-aid caravan and there were 70 casualties, of whom 35 were serious. I saw one man semi-conscious, with blood pouring from his head and neck. Fortunately there were two doctors there. I saw a young boy outside the caravan trembling with fear because he had been attacked by police while he was simply standing with his dad. There was a woman in a terrible state because she had got separated from her son. It was clear that not only*

would the police not allow an ambulance to come near the first-aid caravan to pick up the casualties but that they were running around the caravan and the bus, chasing people and creating casualties.

...It was horrific. I couldn't believe it—the absolute horror of standing in the middle of the night in the middle of London, seeing the police flailing about with their truncheons at people who only a moment earlier had been standing talking, and to know it was authorised and planned. Everyone was involved, from people in their sixties to young children..."

8 A SPIRITUAL JOURNEY

Between the ages of 15 and 16 I felt like a square peg in a round hole. I couldn't get along with Christianity. Sometime later in my life I saw an interview by John Freeman with Carl Jung, the famous psychiatrist. In that interview John Freeman asked, "Mr Jung, can you tell us about your belief in God?"

"I don't believe in God," replied Jung. Freeman, visibly thrown, said, "Surely, Mr Jung, you have written all these books about religious experiences and yet you say you don't believe in God?"

"That's right," said Jung with a twinkle in his eye, "I don't believe." He paused dramatically, and then said, "I know."

From that moment I wanted to know God through my own experience, not by believing. It was then I started to go to different spiritual leaders and read books about spirituality.

When Maharishi Mahesh Yogi came to London for the first time I went to see him at the Hilton Hotel in Park Lane. I was very struck by him, so I suppose my spiritual life started with my induction into transcendental meditation. The induction ceremony involved going to Eaton Square where the Yogi was staying at that time. I had to take a bunch of flowers, a white handkerchief and a piece of fruit. I took an apple. I also had to write down on a piece of paper why I had come and what I wanted. This was given to the Yogi who was sitting in his white robes. He smiled gently and gave me a mantra that was never to be said to anyone else.

I found all of this very helpful and the experiences were like nothing I had ever had before. Still, after a period of years with transcendental meditation I started feeling uncomfortable. I kept up the meditation for some time but not as rigidly every day as I had done in the first few years. It somehow made me too sensitive in dealing with the harshness of the world outside in my work at that time as a union official in the strife-torn print industry.

Some years later I was training as a counsellor at the Herts and Beds Pastoral Foundation, in a huge gothic cathedral near London Colney in Hertfordshire. I used to deliver my papers all night and then go straight to the course at 9am until 1pm. Only then did I go home to sleep.

It was a condition of the course that I had to find a therapist and on one occasion when I arrived too early in Great Gaddeson to see my therapist I decided to drive around the country lanes. It was then I caught my first glimpse of the Amaravati Buddhist Centre.

I loved the place immediately and spoke to the leading monk, Ajahn Sumedho. I remember being struck by his large face. In fact everything about him was large. He stood approximately 6ft 2"—a powerful presence with much authority—and had a great American accent. He had been in the American Peace Corp in the 1950s Korean War.

Ajahn Sumedho was a monk of the Theravadan Thai Forest tradition. He commanded attention, his voice seeming to rumble from deep within him. He was kind, sometimes gentle, and sometimes fierce, with a great sense of humour.

When we were in conversation early on he asked me about my life.

"It's strange sitting here talking to you, a Buddhist monk," I remarked.

"Why?" he enquired with smiling eyes.

"Well, when I was a child at nursery I used to be quite content just to sit cross-legged for long periods. One day the lady in charge noticed me and gave me the nickname 'Buddha Wooder' which stuck, as nicknames do." He chuckled loudly at this. "Buddha Wooder eh? I like that."

He teased me a bit, to my embarrassment. Then I relaxed and we laughed together as it was very clear to both of us that I had no illusions of grandeur. He has called me Buddha Wooder ever since.

I recall a later occasion, after I became a Buddhist, when my wife and I were off on a holiday to the Canaries, waiting at Luton Airport for our flight at 5.30 in the morning. I became aware of a group of tall monks, about six in all, including Ajahn Sumedho. He spotted me first, and his deep resonant voice boomed out around the airport lounge, "Ah, Buddha Wooder!" Some of the other monks looked at me slightly puzzled. Ajahn was really chuckling and enjoying my reaction.

"How are you?" we asked simultaneously.

"Fine," I replied and introduced him. "This is my wife Joy."

Ajahn responded by introducing the remaining monks and explained, "We're off to Sweden for a conference." My wife's face was a picture as she processed the situation.

"That will be nice," I heard her say in what I think is one of the greatest cockney accents in London. Ajahn smiled and I caught his quick penetrating glance as if he was taking in a great deal about my wife in that moment.

It was time for their plane and we all said goodbye.

"Weren't they nice, Bern?" chirped my wife as the monks glided off, almost in formation, to their terminal.

"Yes, they are," I said, and reflected, "That's one of the reasons I became a Buddhist."

When I had first met Ajahn Sumedho he told me there were Saturday morning classes in Buddhist meditation, and had recommended that I do a retreat. So after just two weeks of Buddhist meditation classes I booked in for a 14-day silent retreat.

I remember the first retreat as if it were yesterday. The weather was beautiful and you could hear the wind chimes everywhere. It was an idyllic setting with huge trees that creaked as they swayed in the breeze and there were many varieties of birds and wildlife. But after two or three days my mind started to wander. I asked myself what I was doing there in the silence, repeatedly alternating an hour's meditation while sitting down with an hour's meditation while walking. Why wasn't I in a pub having a pint? Why wasn't I at home having a laugh with my family? I must be mad to be there.

My mind raced round and round but I stayed with it, resisting all temptation to leave as some people did. On the fourth day I was meditating, sitting down in the big hall, when I experienced the most beautiful feelings of liquid love flowing through my veins: feelings so deep, so healing, so nurturing, that even now as I remember, I still have a tendril of connection to them.

This was it—the most incredible experience of my life. I *knew* God rather than *believed*. And other aspects of this experience grew stronger each day. I could watch my mind flip dementedly from one thing to another to find eventually a place of such security and peace that it was a revelation in itself. To think I trusted that mind! The Indians got it so right with their Monkey God as a representation of how the mind jumps constantly from one thing to another. I was part of this great stillness, this great oneness that interconnected everyone and everything, every tree, every blade of grass, every bead of early morning dew. Everything was one in a sense of stillness and an eternal 'now'.

I found this first retreat such a life-changing experience that a couple of retreats a year became a regular part of my life. Each time I came away with something broader, deeper and different. I gained new insights, feelings, a stronger sense of wellbeing, and a clarity of thinking as though my mind had been cleansed.

I had been trying to find a Buddhist psychotherapy training, but until now had not found one. And the strangest thing happened: at the end of a silent retreat you are allowed to talk, and I turned to a woman sitting next to me, we introduced ourselves, and I said I was having trouble finding a Buddhist psychotherapy training. To my amazement she said she was just starting such a training; it was in Devon, was called Karuna, and she gave me their phone number. Was this just a coincidence?

9 BUDDHISM – THE DEFINING RETREAT

I woke up and glanced at the clock. It was 4.33am and pitch black outside. I was lying in bed at the Buddhist retreat in Hertfordshire. I tried to get up to go to the toilet and suddenly felt a searing pain through my back and leg. I shifted position but the pain got worse. I broke out into a sweat, hardly able to move. It was serious and I felt very frightened. All I could think was that I would be unable to work and pay the mortgage. I lay in bed frozen by the pain and wondered what the hell I was going to do.

A month earlier I had hurt my back one evening at work on the newspaper. Our proprietor Rupert Murdoch had moved his operations to Wapping, making many workers redundant, and this had the effect of doubling up the loads of papers that we took out for delivery. One night I went to swing a particularly heavy bundle and felt a terrible pain in my back. Towards the end of the following week it had eased a little, but now I knew I was still in trouble.

I lay in the darkness, thinking. I knew my injury meant I would lose my job and my only source of income. My whole change of career rested on attending a three and a half year Buddhist psychotherapy training course in Devon, due to start a few months later. What if I couldn't go? Not only would I have no money, but I also wouldn't be able to do the necessary studies for my career change. I was a 50 year-old man with no degree, and because of my back problem, now unable to do any form of manual work. Who would be interested in offering me a job? My whole future seemed to be finished before it had even started.

I peered around the dormitory window having only the moonlight to help me to see where I was going. I limped along, bending my body over to the left in an attempt to ease the sickening pain down my right side and across the base of my back.

With each movement I was struggling to find a way to lessen the breath-catching pain and—for some odd reason—trying not to disturb other people. I desperately wanted to avoid being stared at and seen looking so vulnerable. The only sound was of men snoring. All were strangers to me as there had been no time to form any contact in this silent retreat.

Being in this strange place, with thirty men I didn't know, exaggerated my feelings of disorientation and vulnerability. I made my way to the retreat door and managed to limp outside. I slipped on the icy floor but managed to grab a snow-covered tree branch. The sudden jolt of slipping sent another agonising pain through my right leg and across my lower back. I started to cry quietly, the tears freezing on my face.

Faced with this pain I gradually became aware there was much more to me than I'd ever imagined. I could observe my turbulent thoughts and feel the emotions and was able to observe my mind going here, there and everywhere but from a still point. Up until that point I'd been under the illusion that I was in charge of managing and running my life, with career changes planned at certain points. But when I was struck down, made redundant and left practically disabled I realised I was at the mercy of what happened in my life and, even more importantly, that I always had been. I had to trust and hope everything would come right and that I would find an answer.

Even though I was in so much pain I felt that if Buddhism was worth anything this was my time to find out. So I limped through the walking meditation which just happened to be in the pouring rain, determined I was not going to give up.

As I was finishing one phase of walking meditation, I looked up and saw Ajahn Sumedho watching me through the window of a retreat hut. When I finished the walking meditation he came up to me and said I possessed the kind of determination that was rare in the West—the kind it took to become enlightened—and that many people at the retreat faced with my pain would have gone home. He said, "You are a remarkable man Mr Wooder." His words were incredibly helpful; and just that he had noticed and watched me had a profound effect on me.

I decided to take the opportunity of the space the retreat offered me and the circumstances of this crisis to explore myself in the deepest possible way. I faced a whole range of emotions during the following fourteen days. Sitting cross-legged in the retreat intensified the pain; yet something about the levels of physical pain, mental anguish and frustration I'd reached gave me a sense of greater strength and depth.

Staying became a rite of passage. Day in, day out, I was in extraordinary pain yet, although I felt angry and panicky about my responsibilities and wondered why this had happened to me, I still managed to study and meditate. I came out of the retreat a changed person, having experienced what many cultures put their men through, *a coming of age*. I realised I had put myself through a self-imposed initiation.

I meditated on my situation, letting all the angry emotions and images flood through me until they were spent. What I learnt about myself and human nature was a deeply humbling experience.

I allowed myself to be open to every feeling, every thought and every sensation; and this led me to experience what Joseph Conrad called *The Heart of Darkness*. The rage that surged through me endlessly hour after hour was accompanied by monstrous images from my unconscious mind. One moment I was a lion in the Masai Mara, feeding, tearing right inside the carcass of a zebra; the next moment I was invaded by the most profane and pornographic images. I sometimes felt I was losing touch with my humanity and that I should stop this deep, unflinching enquiry.

Then I would hear a bird sing, smell the dew, feel the cool damp mist on my face, breathe in the cold pure air. It was such a huge contrast—every one of my senses felt cleansed so that I became very much more aware and receptive. I became the quietness behind the countryside and all its noises, the silent stillness and space between objects, like trees, birds and rocks. I felt a oneness of nurturing connection with all things, and this extended into feelings of safety, trust and knowing sureness.

I realised I had witnessed the Ego's unremitting battle for its life, for supremacy, but I also understood that just a little contact with being, the divine, a glimpse of enlightenment, can go a very long way. I came out of the retreat a changed person.

The prospect of seeing my family was fantastic yet tinged with anxiety about what their concern for me might be. Then there was the adjustment to the reality of being in the world—and driving, with the added pain of my back.

Every time I had to brake on my slow drive home the searing pain would shoot from my ankle to my mid back, so intense that it was difficult for me to concentrate on the traffic. Changing gears and negotiating roundabouts was a nightmare. When I arrived home my wife's face was full of anxiety as she could see I was really hurt. My children were running around trying to help, taking my case, and I was surrounded by all the love and concern you could possibly have; but nothing could touch this pain.

Things seemed to go wrong all together. My wife had arranged to see a friend and I took her because I didn't want to disappoint her after being away for fourteen days. But I was in agony all evening, greatly relieved when we finally left. It is somehow better being in agony in your own home.

I arrived back and was drinking a cup of tea and managing to get my leg and back comfortable when I heard the key in the lock. My daughter came in, looking very worried, to say she and her boyfriend had been chased and nearly driven off the road by a local gang. Her boyfriend was still outside in the car, too frightened to get out because the gang was in another car waiting for him. I hobbled out in pain, somehow knowing they wouldn't start trouble with me, and brought the boyfriend in as the gang shouted they would get him later.

Anxiety about my daughter's safety was the last thing I needed when I was in such physical pain. I was home now but there was no rest. I felt like the gods were turning the screw on me. *What do I have to learn from this?* I kept thinking. The Buddhist answer would be to become less attached and meditate more.

10 THE PROCESS
OF HEALING

My concerns about being made redundant because of my back injury were somewhat alleviated when I learnt that my firm was going to keep me on full pay for a couple of months. This came as a great relief as it gave me time to see what was now possible in my life.

The main priority was dealing with the pain and healing my back. While I was attending the physiotherapy clinic at Barnet the consultant informed me that I had crushed two discs in my spine. They could not operate because I was too overweight, which made any operation much more potentially dangerous.

While part of me would have done anything to be rid of the pain, I was in some ways very relieved that an operation on my spine was not possible. It is such an important and delicate area that if any operation had gone wrong I could, as the consultant warned, have been left totally paralysed. Intensive physiotherapy was recommended, some of which proved marginally beneficial.

A very good friend of mine, Dr Milton Samanowitz, who had also suffered a back injury early in his life, advised me to lie flat on the floor with three or four books under my head until the level was right. That simple advice, based on his experiences and on his training in the Alexander technique, was most helpful. Packs of frozen peas to numb the pain and eventually traction also aided the process.

I was very nervous of the traction. It consisted of lying on a table that parted in the middle with a leather belt around the top part of the body and another around the bottom part. The belts got tighter and tighter as the table gradually opened and brought about the traction on the lower spine as the hips and legs were pulled in opposite directions. This exercise was designed to help the discs to free up the nerve they were crushing—the cause of so much pain.

Gradually, after months of visits and exercises, it eased a little. Then one day when I was on the traction it eased considerably. I paused the traction, which was controlled manually, and the physiotherapist came to me to ask if I was OK.

"Absolutely fine," I said, "the pain has eased dramatically."

The following week I had to go for further x-rays to check my progress since traction. The x-rays revealed that the crushed discs were still pinching the nerve, though not as much as before. So I was back for more traction. Yet as the machine started to work one day I was so concerned about interfering with the level of comfort that I had now reached that I decided there and then not to continue with any more traction. The physiotherapist tried to dissuade me, saying we could still make my back that much better; but I had made up my mind.

"No, I want to stop," I insisted. Then the strangest thing happened: the leather belt on the traction machine snapped. The physiotherapist looked worried and said to me, "Well that's because you are so overweight, Mr Wooder." I took it as a sign that maybe the gods were now looking after me and never went back to physiotherapy or the hospital. Nevertheless I am, and will always remain, very grateful for the care I received there, and am even more grateful to my friend Milton Samonowitz who had, in fact, advised against traction.

Meanwhile, as I went on receiving pay from work, there were visits from managers to verify that I was at home and was genuinely injured. These visits were very worrying because they were always carried out with a veneer of friendliness but with an underlying feeling of suspicion. It always made me feel very angry to be in such a vulnerable and powerless position, in need of their approval for the continuance of my wages. This was the context in which I made the decision to go to the Karuna Institute to train as a therapist.

I practiced my meditation which helped at times. There is a lot of stoicism needed in Buddhism but when it did help it was miraculous in every sense.

On one occasion I remember being in great pain about 3am. My family were all asleep and so, it seemed when I looked out of the window, was almost everyone else. I felt isolated and in despair, wondering what I could do about my continual pain. Then I decided to meditate.

Buddhists meditate on the pain; but that just seemed to make it worse, more intense and tortuous. Tears of frustration and agony welled up inside me. I railed against Buddhism, just when I needed help so much, feeling emotionally and physically exhausted. My watch showed that 43 minutes had gone by, and I decided to give up my attempts at meditation for the time being.

At that moment a huge wave of soft peace enveloped my whole body. I was totally bewildered but I was going just to enjoy it. My pain seemed to melt into tears of bliss that rolled down my face while warm soft energy floated through my whole body, lovingly soothing the pain. I had been wondering how this incredible experience had come about and now, without thinking, I found the answer. I had finally and completely surrendered. I had thought I had surrendered before but this was total. Emotionally and physically there was nothing left but peace.

Following this moment of surrender, my compassion grew for my family, my friends, all of us in fact who share this stunningly beautiful planet. This was a great personal breakthrough, a treasure in my life beyond compare. It gave me a more comprehensive and deeper empathy for my clients and for the characters in movies. It helped me to take nothing for granted. I saw how lucky I was with my family and my life in general and understood that in the final analysis there are no guarantees, no rights in life—only how it is.

A few days following my incredible experience with the meditation on my back pain, my mind was drawn back to what happened. How, when fed up and angry, I gave up meditating, I was suddenly infused with that wonderful healing experience. I know I surrendered but I didn't do so consciously. But I did consciously give up meditating. I can only conclude that in the moment of giving up, I had opened up enough space to find myself in a state of grace.

At this point something mysterious happened because you cannot consciously surrender. By that I mean you cannot control your autonomic nervous system. For example you cannot make the hairs on your arms stand up on command, you cannot order yourself to blush and instantly turn red. So when my ego stopped trying, it allowed a shift to another level of consciousness where these experiences can happen. The essence is of letting go so totally and deeply that there is not one scintilla of ego in the way, thus allowing such an alignment to take place.

11 BECOMING A THERAPIST

I had thought I would be too unwell to attend the Buddhist psychotherapy course in at the Karuna institute in Devon, and after coming to terms with my back pain, I rang the director, Maura Sills, to explain that I would be unable to attend. She was kindness itself and asked if someone who lived quite near me could pick me up, and whether I could lie in the back of the camper van. I agreed to try. I will always be grateful to Tom Greaves and Tony Farley for their remarkable kindness in taking me down to Devon and back.

I felt incredibly nervous because I could hardly move and I found it a terrifying prospect to travel all that way with snow on the road. Through my mind flashed thoughts about what I would do if we had a breakdown or crash before I had even started the first of the monthly courses. I knew that if we got into difficulties I couldn't get out and help to push. I was used to driving myself and now I was totally dependent on others—subject to their arrangements and moods.

Still, the journeys down to the course at Karuna, in Totnes, were like PhD seminars in themselves. Tony had been to Cambridge where he had studied criminology and Tom had graduated with a philosophy degree. Tom dominated a room with his presence and had a brilliant mind.

We came to psychotherapy from different backgrounds and different intellectual levels, so our individual perspectives on therapy and our mix of moods and personalities made those four-hour journeys absolutely fascinating. In fact I count them among some of my richest experiences. The topics that came up, the memories, the happiness, the pain, the sadness—all of these emotions were brought to the surface by Karuna.

Our journeys could also be very funny, with Tom getting apoplectic about people towing caravans.

"Look, look, look at this bloke in front," he would cry, starting his regular lament about caravans. "He's going too fast... the wind will catch it...ooh told you, he was lucky that time, it nearly went... I am getting away from this bloke." Tony would quietly grin at me as we both watched Tom's war dance. Tom would realise and roar with laughter giving Tony a friendly shove. Tony would laugh and say, "There, there, Tom."

I would say, "Tom, you need a couple of missiles on the front of the van to fire at will." Tom would respond, "I like that. Yeah, I'll give it to 'em, those caravans".

There was a great bond between Tony and Tom. They were really good friends, with complimentary personalities. Tony was the quieter of the two, thoughtful, logical, very sharp and humorous. Tom was an explosion of personality, observations and insights. He reminded me of a temperamental artist, encompassing a mass of contradictions. On the one hand he could demonstrate a fast, shrewd business mind, and sometimes be extremely aggressive; while on the other he could be very gentle.

During the journeys the mood would go quiet and I would become reflective. I would watch the fields go by, trying in vain to get my back comfortable, feeling restless, bored and apprehensive about the weekend ahead of us.

At Karuna for the first year, because of my pain, I had to take strong painkillers and listen to the lectures while lying flat on the floor. The weekends at Karuna could be quite daunting and I knew I might have to work as a therapist with someone in the middle of a large group. At the end the group would make observations about how I had worked and what interventions I had made. If I hadn't picked up on something or even noticed it I would be asked why I had not, what that said about me, and whether it was worth my looking at in my own therapy. I wondered anxiously if I would be OK.

I felt different from the others because I was the oldest there bar one and because I was among university graduates. As a boy who had left school at fifteen, I found it very strange to be in a group where all the other people had been to university. They came from similar backgrounds, shared an understanding and a way of talking, and had been through similar experiences. It remained unsaid but I knew that I was outside of that. I had to find my way and cut through a lot of conditioning to stay, because at times I felt very inferior. However, I was glad I hung on in there: it was an amazing experience and I met some fascinating people.

This was the only Buddhist psychotherapy course in the country. It consisted of a six month introductory training period at the end of which, if you were accepted as eligible, you could go on to take the full three-year professional psychotherapy training course at Dartington Hall, Totnes.

This three-year training consisted of eleven long week-ends a year, starting on Friday evenings at 7pm and ending about mid-day on Sunday, plus one residential week per year. We studied specialist books on Buddhism, and on Freud, Jung, Reich, Wilbur and many others; every year we had to produce three or four substantial essays.

There were predominantly experiential weekends where we got to know ourselves in the group therapy sessions and examined how we interacted with each other. In the case of those with whom we did not interact well, we were asked to look at what got in the way of that.

Other sessions consisted of lectures on different topics with questions and answers afterwards. One topic, for example, was *the body and how it holds the memory of emotion*. Sometimes monks would be invited to give a lecture and one year there was a series of talks by a psychiatrist.

At the end of each year we were asked to provide a self-assessment paper and an assessment of two of our peers. It was very helpful finding out if there was a common theme in the peer assessments. They gave us a guide as to how our gifts and qualities were perceived and which areas we needed to work on. Like Buddhism, it was a very balanced approach—one that suited me well.

Sometimes we looked at different personality types such as people with borderline personality disorders, depression etc, and how to work with them. The question and answer sessions that followed took our understanding (or sometimes our confusion) further, but we were able to turn to our books to clarify and build on what we were learning.

I was exploring a part of myself as never before, finding the warmth and space to develop and be myself among fellow trainees with such diverse backgrounds, education and beliefs. For me they were fascinating people with brilliant minds whose quiet, subtle personalities could open you up.

Some were gifted in other ways: they could touch you physically in a place they felt intuitively drawn to and the effect on you would be incredible. They had the ability to know where you held repressed emotion in your body.

One day I was waiting to go to the group meeting at Karuna and had just finished my tea in the old kitchen when I saw Franklyn Sills coming towards the kitchen. He just frowned slightly and with four fingers outstretched, palm down, touched my throat and asked "What's going on there?" With that I started to feel choked up with emotion and a memory came to me of being in hospital.

Looking back on this incident I am still amazed both by Franklyn's perception and the fact that such a simple touch could be so powerful.

"I don't know," I said. He was smiling calmly.

"Good place for you to work with." I agreed, experiencing some sense of release from emotional tension which up to that point I hadn't even known I was carrying.

ROMANTIC STORY

Franklyn and Maura Sills ran Karuna together. Franklyn, an American who had been a monk in Thailand, had met Maura who had been a Buddhist nun when they were both part of the same order. They fell in love, decided to leave the order and finally got married, but carried on their spiritual development and work by starting Karuna and core process psychotherapy.

At Karuna I quickly broadened my appreciation of the amazing spectrum of different approaches, talents and qualities of those around me. The atmosphere could be loving, safe and magic just as it could be disconcerting and frightening. We gained both helpful and painful insights, maturing and opening up on so many levels as we forged relationships. Tom said to me, "Bernie, you have a personality made of girders."

Maura sat in our circle of coloured cushions and told us what we were going to do each morning. Her soft Scottish accent was so attractive and comforting that everyone held on to her every word. The sun streamed in through the huge windows and made rainbows on the carpet while the incense wafted across the room and danced in grey circles of smoke. Somehow everyone could be seen more clearly when they were lost in attention.

I would survey the group, and take in the personalities of my peers. First there was Margaret, who had been a social worker for twenty five years, and was a balance of calm authority and spirituality. She had cornflower blue eyes, and resembled the actress June Whitfield, but was more stately in her manner and walk. Another wise friend—we are still in touch.

Anthony was a gentle giant: soft spoken, a sincere and committed Buddhist. He had a voice that could soothe and reassure by its tone alone. His care for people was palpable.

Miranda, a very sharp ex lawyer with shrewd blue eyes, would be analysing and sifting every word. You knew that later she would make some interesting comment or put a question with such clarity and intelligence that it would make you more aware.

I met Jan on the introductory six months' training in London and we got on from the start. Jan had been a director at Sotheby's but decided on a change of career and direction. She was an unusual balance of scientist and mystic, an experienced Buddhist. She had a husky, breathy voice which gave her what I can only describe as a misty quality. She has been a great supportive friend ever since.

On one occasion during Maura's lecture I caught my breath and suddenly felt a searing pain through my whole body as I lay there. I thought *I must remember not to shift position too quickly because it hurts so much. Where are my painkillers?*

My attention went back to Maura who was saying, "Now the body remembers emotion: it has cellular memory in which it is all stored. Franklyn is amazing at this work." I remembered the day I had evidence of that with him in the kitchen.

We also worked in groups of three where one would be the therapist, one the client, and one the observer of both therapist and client. It was not role play, as the person being the client would talk about real issues in their lives. I valued this more than anything else at Karuna because I prefer the whole idea of regular experiential learning.

Our learning was reinforced, when we came back from these monthly training weekends, by having to form a peer group and meet each week to do what were called exchanges. The exchanges involved working as therapist, client and observer, following the same model as at Karuna.

These weekly exchanges deepened our confidence and experience of being the therapist, our self discovery by being the client, and the special skills involved in being an observer of both therapist and client working together. For example, as the therapist gained understanding and empathy for the client, we could observe how the therapist's body language began to match how the client was sitting. The facial expressions of the client and whether their breathing was shallow, fast or if they were holding their breath, were all extremely important indicators for the therapist, apart from the content of the conversation itself.

12 LIFE AT THE SHARP END

I decided that I was not going to sit at home and wait for experience to come to me, so I applied for three placements. I worked for the mental health charity Mind in Finchley for about a year and for a similar period at John Scotts Family Clinic (an annex of Barts Hospital), where I saw the parents and the other therapists saw the children. At the same time I had a placement at the Whittington Community Psychiatric Clinic in Finsbury, and it was here I met Chloe with whom I was asked to run a group for carers. Interestingly , they did not want therapy, or to look at anything difficult, but just wanted a cup of tea and a chat with people sharing the same experiences.

It was a period in which I learnt to find myself as a therapist. I was exposed to a variety of therapists of different orientations who gave me supervision. In this way I gained a great deal of practical experience of the different developmental models of psychotherapy that I had studied during my training. I also had the opportunity of working with clients who were dealing with range of problems including depression, acute anxiety, sexual abuse or marital difficulties. Eventually, however, I realised that you have to let go of everything that you have been taught—

just trust yourself—and then all you have been taught comes through. It takes time to have the confidence to do that and it was a real 'growth' experience for me.

MIND

When I first went to Mind I was struck by the comfort of the place. It was a large house with about five client rooms near Tally Ho Corner. I would attend a group meeting with another four counsellors and new clients seeking counsellors would be presented to find out when they could be seen and by whom. The assessment counsellor would present her assessment of their needs. A discussion would then follow and efforts would be made to match as far as possible a counsellor with special experience, say with addiction or sexual abuse, to the client's needs.

This is where I first met Chloe. We worked together in a group for carers who, interestingly, did not want therapy, but just cups of tea and a laugh and chat with people in similar circumstances. Chloe is a very nice person and I found her a careful, interesting therapist. She has a keen sense of humour, with alive, expressive brown eyes; she has a wide interest in the arts—painting in particular—and is a compassionate, empathic person. She now lives in Greece, and I miss her.

JOHN SCOTTS FAMILY CLINIC

As I drove to John Scotts Family Clinic past Finsbury Park I was struck by the buzz of the area. I went to the clinic reception and asked the friendly woman there for Jonathan Bradley. Down the stairs came a very tall man, hand extended. As we shook hands I was still looking up and up. I think he must have been about 6' 6" while I am 5' 2". You notice these things, especially up close.

After I started my placement at John Scotts I would arrive at 9am and go upstairs to look at the notice board. On it would be a programme for the day, meetings, briefings etc with a note of who was to attend each one written alongside in brackets. I would check for my name and it would read '2pm multi-disciplinary, Bernie to attend'. The multi-disciplinary meeting would normally involve social workers and therapists along with GPs and psychiatrists, plus advocates and interpreters. There would be reports presented, all problems thoroughly thought through and discussed, then actions decided with recommendations from the therapist concerned.

I sat there sometimes in sheer disbelief to hear of the level of suffering in some families. I learnt about the culture of abuse in all its forms, noting how often patterns repeated themselves and how often the same problem was handed down from generation to generation. I was also deeply impressed by the sheer courage, tenacity to survive and determination to be rid of this suffering by the families attending the clinic. Their stories could arouse powerful reactions in me—fury, sadness, despair, inspiration and often humour.

THE WHITTINGTON
COMMUNITY PSYCHIATRIC CLINIC

It was so strange walking up to the entrance of the Whittington Community Psychiatric Clinic—the Pine Street Clinic as I once knew it. It was near where we used to live when I was a child and memories began flooding back.

As a baby I had been taken to be weighed and immunized at Pine Street clinic. Recalling that my Nan had lived right opposite, I turned automatically to look for her house, but of course the building was no longer there. But here I was, 55 years later, walking in as a psychotherapist.

It made me realise what a journey my life had been. I was born into war and for the first six years of my life had known chaos, panic and fear, but also community, kindness and humour. In some ways it was not so surprising that I had become a psychotherapist.

I heard myself say, "Mr Wooder to see Dr Hollander," and was directed towards the first door on my right. I moved towards it, still partly lost in the memories and atmosphere of the place.

"Come in," said a voice in response to my knock. Dr Hollander was a lady of about fifty sitting at a desk, her glasses on a long chain round her neck. She had a broad, strong face and was smiling at me.

"Mr Wooder, please come and sit down and tell me about yourself and your training."

I explained that I had completed three years of counselling training at Herts, Beds and Bucks Pastoral Centre, then a further three and half years' psychotherapy training at Karuna.

"Karuna," she said, suddenly more interested. "Tell me about it."

"Well, it's psychotherapy training really, bringing together Buddhist psychology with western developmental models of psychotherapy." Dr Hollander raised her eyebrows.

"Oh, it's interesting that you trained as a counsellor as well. What model was the counselling?"

"It was predominantly psychodynamic," I replied.

"Ok, I'll confer with Jim, our resident psychiatrist, and I'll contact you. How did you find the journey down here: I mean, would it be alright for you?"

"Well actually, Dr Hollander," I began, "it's brought back so many memories for me. I was born and brought up in this area. This was the actual clinic where I was brought to be weighed and immunised as a baby, and where my mum used to come and collect my cod liver oil tablets, malt and orange juice."

At this Dr Hollander lit up.

"Oh, it's invaluable that you are of the local culture Bernie. When can you start?" I was a bit confused at this point.

"Don't you need me to see Jim first?"

"No," she said, "don't worry about that."

Before I could reply she asked, "Can you start Wednesday?" I said I could.

"Good, see you at 9 o'clock and have a chat with Jim," she beamed. She was delightfully eccentric.

I walked into Jim's office to find him looking very tired and for a moment I wondered what I had let myself in for.

My first week working with Dr Hollander was interesting to say the least. She answered her phone on one occasion and listened with an intense look of concentration.

"OK, OK, I'll be there," she said authoritatively and put the phone down. She faced me, looking excited.

"Bernie, you must come with me. A man has just hung himself and you have to have the experience—it will be good for you." The image of a man hanging immediately flashed across my mind with the simultaneous thought *how could this be good for me?* But this was life at the sharp end of psychiatry in London at that time.

At that point an emergency case came in, a very anxious couple in their fifties, one of whom, the woman, had experienced some disturbing psychotic episode on a train.

"Bernie will deal with you," Dr Hollander boomed with warmth and confidence.

When the husband asked if he could come in to see me with his wife, my eyes met those of Dr Hollander, who was still beaming.

"No, I think it would be best if you wait out here," I heard myself say with authority. It was amazing, the speed of thought and intuition that preceded those instant decisions. My simple reasoning was that sometimes people don't want to talk in front of their loved ones for a variety of reasons, out of protection or due to intimate disclosures. At any rate, my decision turned out to be the right one; but consequently I did not see the hanged man.

I tell the above story because it gives an insight into the kind of atmosphere and circumstances I found myself in during this baptism of becoming a psychotherapist. I discovered many different approaches and how many different kinds of people there are.

I also learnt an incredible amount about *my* own presumptions and assumptions. I had assumed that all standards in families were the same and it came as a great surprise to me to discover that they were not.

Behind every person's actions, however pointless they may seem, lies a story and a reason why they make their judgment in a particular way. I found it gave me much more humility and much greater compassion as I came to understand this. It was a real journey for me.

Gradually, through working in the different placements, I built up the four hundred client hours with supervision that are required for accreditation as a professional psychotherapist with the United Kingdom Council for Psychotherapists (UKCP). The experience also strengthened my confidence.

A funny thing happened: I had just finished my last client and was walking through the clinic with Dr Hollander, when I saw to my amazement my mum sitting in reception and telling the receptionist that "It's ok, my son's a psychotherapist here. And"—with an air of grandness—"he's taking me to dinner!" She announced it as if we were going to a posh restaurant. We did in fact go to Mansi's pie and mash shop in Exmouth Market. While this was going on, Dr Hollander had been amused at my embarrassment.

Meanwhile my private practice was beginning to build up. All I had to do now was complete my ten thousand-word thesis on my theoretical understanding of my three and a half years' training, and how I had put that training into practice in working with clients in the placements.

My thesis *On Becoming A Therapist* was an opportunity to communicate all that I had learnt in life, on the course at Karuna, and in working in the placements. It was also a way of bringing to the fore my understanding of the different models of psychotherapy and my experience of working with them.

Preparing my thesis and tackling the difficult questions it brought up in me showed me where I was and where I needed to focus my attention further. It was a very productive and helpful exercise—an investigation, an audit of the depth of my knowledge and understanding.

It was an enormous psychological relief to empty myself of all of that and to gain a snapshot of Bernie Wooder the psychotherapist, so I think my title and subject matter were extremely well chosen and still serve me today.

I prepared my thesis with Jonathan Stock, whose name was given to me as a core process psychotherapist who lived locally, and with whom I could exchange the roles of therapist and client.

When I arrived at Jonathan's home in Finchley I was met by a man with a huge, very striking shock of black wavy hair. I said, "Hello, are you Jonathan?"

"Yes, I am," he replied in a very cultured voice.

I said, "I'm Bernie. I've come to have exchanges and some supervision with you." As he extended his hand I noticed his eyes were dark brown and his skin very white. He looked physically frail and vulnerable but the strength was in his head and face.

We set up a procedure whereby Jonathan would ask me penetrating questions about my knowledge of the psychotherapy of Freud, Jung, Wilbur and Mazlow and my experiences in my placements. He would write down my answers, leaving me free to think. I have always found this method of working the most effective in bringing forth the depth of my knowledge.

Jonathan had an extremely sharp mind and would throw in his own questions, prompting me to reveal a greater depth and knowledge than I realised I had.

I will be eternally grateful to him. I think he was the most intelligent and cultured man I had ever met. He was incredibly well read, had followed the Indian guru Osho and had lived in Poona, India, for some time. He left an indelible impression on me not only because of his cultured voice, fine mind and capacity for analysis but also because I felt he had known great suffering.

He was to tell me later about South Africa. He said to me one day, "Bernie, it's so interesting for me to meet a cockney like you." I was somewhat surprised at this and asked why.

"Well, my dad was a cockney from the East End who emigrated to South Africa. You share many similarities in attitude, build and accent."

"Oh," I said. He just smiled. He had a great smile which lit up his whole face but it was odd because as the smile faded his face would take on a look of melancholy. He was a kind of Dickensian character with something tragic about him.

As we talked one winter's day in Jonathan's dingy flat with a two-bar electric fire on for warmth and the snow falling outside, I asked him how he had come to leave the sunshine of South Africa. He said he had been conscripted into the South African Army and after being promoted to the rank of officer had seen action in Angola. The atrocities he had witnessed there and the political philosophy of his government were things he could no longer tolerate. So he took six weeks leave due to him, bought two air tickets, one ticket to Germany and one to the UK, departing on the same date, and told everyone he was off to Germany for his holidays. The Germany story, though, was just a cover for his real destination—Britain. Unbeknown to

63

the authorities, he had applied some months before for British citizenship, on the basis that his father was a British citizen, and had then purchased another ticket to come here.

Jonathan had remained in the UK for five weeks and then, just as his leave was up, his British citizenship had come through. Now he could stay as a British citizen and he was no longer under the control of the South African government.

"The gods were with me, Bernie: but it was such a bitter-sweet moment."

"Why bitter-sweet?" I asked.

"Well," he replied, "although the citizenship was great, as the holiday period was over my money was running out. I had to find a job quickly, which was very difficult in a new country with no friends, no base, and all the red tape."

13 SOUND OF MUSIC, LOOK OF ROMANCE

MEETING WILL

When I observe therapists in general, I note that they're not often business-minded, and I think the qualities inherent in someone who becomes a therapist are not necessary those conducive to running a business. It was these observations, and a need in myself, that took me on a three-day course in marketing. It was run by an American marketing guru who flew into Heathrow, stayed at the Radisson, and trained us for three to sixteen hour days in marketing. There were approximately three hundred attendees, amongst them a few millionaires.

To the throbbing beat of Eye Of The Tiger, the guru in cream Armani suit walks on; it was exciting and interesting and I loved it. We were asked to get ourselves into groups of eight per table, then you said your line of business and the other seven bombarded you with ideas for your business; you wrote these down and then did it for the next person who told us his or her business.

Having completed this table of eight, you moved on to another group of eight and repeated the process. You did this with as many tables of eight as time allowed, and you ended up with a huge list of business ideas that came from different people in different businesses. The significance of this was to demonstrate that people in a given business think in a certain way in keeping with the culture of that business, but employing this method allowed input from people from another business who, because they were from a different culture. were not limited in their thinking about you.

It was on my first table I met Will. He was Scottish, tall, with mousy hair, and dressed in smart conservative suit. He was very articulate, well mannered, and there was a sensitivity underlying his whole personality. I felt we hit it off more or less straight away.

Afterwards, Will came up to me and asked me some questions, and told me that something I'd said to him had really made him think. He asked for my card, he rang about six weeks later, and we started his therapy.

FIRST SESSION

"Hello Will," I said when he arrived. "How can I help ?"

Will said, "I have a difficult dilemma, which is this: if I do the work necessary to stop me going bankrupt, I will lose my wife."

The fact that his wife was not an immediate priority prompted me to ask, "If you didn't have the business problem, would everything then be ok?" He looked at me for a moment, a bit stunned, then said, "That's an interesting question".

After a period of silence, he said, "Well, my relationship with my wife is not right, and your question made it clearer."

I said, "What has made it clearer?" He shifted around, frowned and said, "I can't seem to do anything right. When I'm at work, she nags me that I'm always at work, and when I'm at home, she attacks me." I said, "When you're at home, say at the breakfast table, what are you thinking about?"

"Work," he said quickly, still completely unaware of how that would feel to his wife.

Realising Will's difficulty in talking about his feelings, and his obvious preoccupation with possible bankruptcy, it was easy to see why his wife felt disconnected from him, and the possible reason for her attacks. I decided to concentrate our work together on his marriage as the priority. His lack of emotional connection to his wife was making him feel very unhappy and isolated in his marriage; yet if ever he needed his wife's support, it was now. I told Will I'd like to do some role play with him.

"How do you feel about that?" I asked him.

"Ok," he said apprehensively.

"I want you to be your wife, and I'll be you." He smiled. "So: the things your wife says to you, just say to me."

I picked up a newspaper from the side of my chair. Will waited, then said, "I'm planning to meet some of the mums at the school."

"Eh?" I mumbled, head down.

Will is now getting into the idea and says, "Did you hear what I said?"

"Yes, good," I mumbled again, still looking at the newspaper.

"I don't know why I talk to you. What's the point? You just don't listen."

Will had got fully into his role as 'his wife', so at that moment I asked, "How do you feel?"

"Annoyed," he answered. "On my own."

"That's why your wife attacks you." He had a 'light bulb' moment and said, "I never realised."

I waited, then thought I would push it further.

"She realises you have a mistress." Will looked shocked and said angrily, "But I don't!"

"But you do," I said firmly. "Her name is Work."

He sat there shocked, but taking in what I had said. I looked at the clock and saw it was time for the session to end. Will left with an air of humility and an understanding of the need to be more emotionally open to his wife.

"Bye Bernie", he said quietly.

At the next session Will came in looking a little calmer, and I asked him how things were going in his marriage after the last session.

"I think it has really helped. We are a bit different now. My wife is still a bit wary of me, but it's made us a little closer."

"Good," I said.

I decided to go back to an earlier remark in which Will had said he liked films.

"Have you a favourite one that moves you emotionally?"

Will looked at me intently; to my surprise, he said, "*The Sound of Music.*"

I was surprised for many reasons, one being that Will was a quiet conservative man and, with his Scottish discipline and sense of masculinity, this film didn't seem at first to fit. I myself don't like the film much, so I asked what he liked about it.

His look softened as he answered, "It's a romantic love story." He said it with a quiet conviction that I'd not see in him before. I probed deeper.

"Could you say if it's the whole film, or a scene or a moment, or the music?"

He flushed a little and said, "It was the moment where Maria's eyes met those of Captain von Trapp across the dance floor." His his voice cracked and tears welled up. I waited as he wiped his eyes and asked, "What was it about that look?" He struggled to find the words.

"It was what passed between them," Tears welled up again.

"Just let them come, Will, don't stop them," I said.

Will looked a little scared, and I felt that he was less used to talking than to listening; but here he was, surprising himself by what he was allowing himself to say. His eyes widened as he continued, "I don't have that in my life." That insight, spoken aloud and with its obvious importance to him, was a major step forward in our work together.

He continued, "I've only just realised how much I need that." He was quiet for some time

"Can you say more, Will?" He cleared his throat.

"The look they exchanged, the mood that was evoked." He was struggling to find the words.

"Will, do you think it was the wordless communication of love that so moved you, and helped you identify what is missing in your life?" He nodded vigorously and more tears came.

"Yes," he said, with a sense of relief.

The room suddenly felt a lot easier and a lot bigger. I was pleased that the film's power had been such a catalyst for Will, and wondered how it would develop following the role play we had done on his marriage.

At a further session Will was less rigid, more relaxed. He sat quietly and then said: "I find it difficult to start conversations. Especially about my feelings."

"So it seems the film helped you do that?" He smiled slightly and said yes. I waited for more and finally prompted him: "Have you thought about the film since?"

He looked down to his right (this was a characteristic he always did when thinking deeply). Then he said something so important.

"I felt about it a lot; the feeling won't leave me." As he said it, he unconsciously touched his tummy; I noted this with interest.

It was a very moving experience for me as he shared this, because I realized its significance. Gradually over the next couple of sessions we were able to get much greater clarity and insight into its connection, to both his marriage and his childhood. It was a catalyst that met and revealed a core need in his personality, and made so much sense of so many things— choices and behaviours, some of which he had until that moment felt very guilty about. Now he was able to understand its root cause, he was able to forgive himself, be at peace and have some compassion for himself.

PIECES OF THE PUZZLE START TO COME TOGETHER

Will came in looking very excited and said, "I've just realized something important. I was watching the DVD of *The Sound of*

Music again, as you asked me to." He was more animated than I had ever seen him. "I now know why that feeling is so important to me."

"Why?" I enquired, as excited as Will was.

"It makes me feel complete," he said.

"Where in your body do you feel that completeness?"

Will looks down at his body, pleased.

"In my chest and tummy," he replies, looking more at peace than I had ever seen him, and suddenly looked younger and stronger again. This was the sort of moment that a psychotherapist never forgets; it signifies the beginning of Will's healing at a deep level, and will change his life.

I said, "Apart from the look, Will, are there any other scenes that moved you or affected you? Any patterns of behaviour?"

Will thought, and said, "Not in the same way; but yes, I identify with his inability to say what he feels."

"Have you always been like that?"

"Yes. Do you know why?" He looked down at his right and gave a big anxious sigh. I had an intuitive flash at this moment, and wondered how Will was experiencing my questions. Prompted by the knowledge that Will does a lot of courses, which have final exam, I said, "Will, you don't have to struggle to get it right. There is no right or wrong, only your experience. I wonder if you experience my questions like an exam?"

Will smiled. "Yes," he said with a real sense of relief.

"Treat them," I suggested, "like a joint exploration with an attitude of curiosity." Will nodded and stretched his legs.

"What happens inside when you go to say something? I want you to see if there's any sensation in your body."

Will looked at me rather quizzically. After a while he said, "My chest."

"Just keep your awareness on your chest," I said. "Let go of any thinking."

A few moments later, he said "My throat, I'm getting sensations there."

"Good, just keep your attention on it." I waited a while, then asked "What's happening?"

"I'm seeing my mum, and three of my brothers around her."

"What are you doing, Will?"

"I'm waiting," he said, looking very sad.

"Waiting for what?"

"To talk to my mum." His voice now sounds much younger. "I can't get her attention, it's frustrating, she's busy getting them ready for school."

He goes silent and still looks sad and resigned.

"What is happening now?"

"I'm walking away," he says, as a tear rolls slowly down his cheek.

Inside I am pleased: Will's body memory has taken us to when he started giving up asking or expressing his needs to his mum. He had become resigned to the fact that his mum had eleven children and there was not much time for him. It had led us to the cause of his trouble in talking about his feelings today.

Time was getting on so I asked him to open his eyes. He took a tissue and wiped his tears.

"How's your throat?"

"It feels different."

"And your chest?" I ventured.

"It feels more free."

Will was quite spaced out as he processed this experiential memory. I just finished with, "Do you think that's where your difficulty talking about your feelings started?"

"Yes," he said quietly, "I think it was."

I let him sit there for a while. Then he got up and said quietly, "See you next week, Bernie."

For a number of sessions I had been teaching Will mindfulness. For those who don't know, it is the Buddhist practice for developing an internal witness or observer that is just aware of your thoughts, feelings and sensations. But this awareness doesn't get sucked in: it just observes.

Will's emotional response to *The Sound of Music* was a pivotal insight that helped many things fall into place. Because in one moment, we were able to link his early, unmet developmental needs to his life now, and their negative impact on the emotional quality of his life: the lost, abandoned child's needs in the adult romantic.

We also discovered, through Will becoming mindful of his bodily responses, where his inability to talk about emotional issues had begun.

I decided to explain to Will about mirroring in a child's early emotional development, and how it helps the adult to have good healthy relationships. The lack of this mirroring was, I felt, at the root of his present emotional insecuritues and the problems he was having with his marriage.

For those who don't know what mirroring is, it is the look in the mother's eyes as she cares for her baby. That look is how the child gains a feeling of his inner sense of self. The way the mother hugs him, plays with him, feeds him, combined with how she physically holds and touches him, will give him his inner sense of self. If he consistently gets looks of warmth, love, smiles, he will feel inside warmth, love, smiling. If however he receives constant looks of anger, anxiety, contempt, he will have a sense of self that is also angry, anxious, self contemptuous.

If that mirroring phase is incomplete, it has a negative effect on the person's adult relationships. And if those needs are not met, that phase of his development will always be needy for its completion, in his life and relationships as an adult.

Will's need for this mirroring manifested in his romantic life, where he was—albeit unconsciously—still looking for that mirror in his wife's eyes. The problem was that she was no longer looking at him romantically, because her own needs were no longer being met.

I noticed over the latter few sessions that Will and his wife were getting closer. His availability to her was much better: the result partly of our role play, and partly of their now joint understanding of Will's difficulties. His wife had been moved by Will's committment to doing something about their marriage problems.

With this in mind, I wondered how to achieve the romantic look, the look that would so help Will and his wife. It would have to be a film that would effect his wife too. Will and I worked out how could he arrange a romantic evening with his wife: something they hadn't had for years. I suggested that they watch *Titanic* before the meal. It would be interesting to see what could happen; and it would be important for Will and his wife specifically to note the looks exchanged between Leonardo de Caprio and Kate Winslet. Will liked our joint venture and decided to do it.

After they had seen the film, and talked about it over in the restaurant, Will came back quite excited. He felt they were making real progress, and reported that his wife was different. They are not there yet, but I feel they have the true beginnings of a relationship that will meet both their emotional needs.

In my desire to see that this case study was as accurate as possible for the book, I asked Will to write in his own words, his experience of our therapy together.

WILL, IN HIS OWN WORDS

The problem I felt I had was that I had a choice. Either a successful business or the failure of my marriage. I felt that the way things were going, these items were mutually exclusive. I couldn't have both, it was one or the other.

This had the effect of isolating me from my wife and family. The business was very new, and as everyone knows, at the start of a new business everything has to be sacrificed in order for the business to be a success. This meant I didn't have anything left over for anyone else. Including me. But even as I spent more and more time with the business I seemed to be getting less and less done.

When I first met Bernie, we were at a business seminar. We had just been posed a challenge. We had to conjure up in our minds a picture of what success would look like. What would it mean to me? I had difficulty in visualising success as it meant thinking in terms of the ultimate choice I would have to make between the two competing goals.

Working with Bernie has helped me to develop ways of dealing with what I felt were two things that could not be reconciled. Over a period of discussions, I began to understand that the person who was deciding that these two goals were mutually exclusive was me. By adopting a different method of dealing with the people and situations involved, I could have both. A successful business and a good marriage.

But it wasn't purely based on the work point of view. I come from a very large family. I know that meant a lot of the rules and control methods were needed to ensure the stability of a large group. However the things that were important and necessary then, may not be required in my life now. In fact they may be positively unhelpful.

In my work with Bernie I came to realise that people live by patterns. They develop patterns based on what they see, encounter, and are influenced by. I was no different. However, as is often the case, when you are very close to the subject, you can't always identify the pattern. If you don't see the pattern that may now be causing the problem, then you don't see the need to change.

Being able to identify patterns that were unhelpful was the key to moving forward.

It wasn't easy. Isn't easy. Bernie suggested watching some movies that may help in identifying something that because it was so close to me, I couldn't see myself. In Secrets and Lies, *the character played by Timothy Spall comes home from work and enters the house tentatively. He doesn't know what to expect or what reception he is going to receive. You can see him moving as if he is trying to pick up the vibes so that he doesn't read the situation wrongly. The film that helped me the most in therapy was* The Sound of Music.

In this I recognised myself. It came from not talking to the person that I needed most to talk to. Oh, we talked all right, about everything except what mattered most. Having been made aware of a pattern was the first step to changing it.

Other films, such as Shirley Valentine, *meant we began to talk about change. A relationship is a living, breathing organism. It is not something that is created many years before and then set in amber, never to change. People do change. What they want and need does change. If no one ever talks about his or her changing lives and feelings, then it is a tacit acceptance that "this is it". This is my life. I must accept it, even if it is draining the life and soul out of me. Well, as the saying goes "if nothing changes, nothing changes".*

I feel that I am able to open a conversation now where before I would have avoided it. It may not be an easy conversation and I may not know how it is going to turn out. But I know I can have the conversation and the world will not come to an end.

In fact I often find out I wasn't the only one thinking this way.

Some months later I contacted Will to see how things were progressing and asked him if he could possibly write about how he saw things now, so I could put it in the book.

I have thought quite a lot about the work we have done, and tried to set out what it felt like, during and after the process. I hope that you will find the following explanation helpful. It really sums up how I feel about what happened and how I feel now.

I was living in the wrong house. It wasn't my fault. It had been built by many other people over a long period of time, thirty six years to be precise. I owned the house but it wasn't mine, it was theirs.

Oh, I occasionally redecorated. Did a bit here, a bit there; but it still wasn't mine. Wasn't me. I didn't like living in it. It was uncomfortable. Didn't fit but I had to live there. I didn't know what else to do. It had after all, always been my home.

Then along came Bernie. He helped me to change the house. But not at all in the way I expected. It wasn't a case of moving to another or different house. It was by rebuilding the one I already owned.

This wasn't going to be easy. I would have to continue living there whilst the work was going on; and of course, I would have to retain a lot of the materials. After all, they were a part of the original house and I owned them. So Bernie helped me demolish the original structure, room by room, timber by timber, brick by brick. Eventually all that was left was the original foundation. To my great surprise, the foundation was actually quite sound. It was fine for building on, if only I knew how to build properly.

14 BUDDHISM AND CATHOLICISM AT THE MOVIES

DISCUSSION BETWEEN PETER MALONE
AND THE AUTHOR

Peter: Bernie, you have a great love of films. You've been watching them since you were very young and now you're using them seriously in your work as a therapist. You use particular sequences to help people respond to and share their experiences. But you also bring your own personal Buddhist appreciation to films. The films are 'the movies'. How do you actually use movies in therapy?

Bernie: It's really the magic moments in the movies. Movies do have moments that touch people, and what I'm doing is pioneering an approach in therapy to look at what it is in those moments, in those particular movies, that touches people. What makes them feel very happy? What makes them feel very sad? What makes them feel very angry? What is it that is making them cry?

When we investigate this it can sometimes be a very small thing, and sometimes it can be the issue of the whole movie. But often it is a moment in the movie that unconsciously triggers a memory, something to do with their own life. There can be a moment when they are discussing a scene in a movie and I am asking them to tell me what the character feels, tell me what they see the character experiencing; and it becomes a moment of transition from the movie experience to their own personal experience. A memory will come back. It could be a song. It could be a memory of being somewhere with someone. They might say to me, "You see what's happening here as these two people are talking in this lounge with the curtains like that? That was exactly the atmosphere that I experienced when I was young. That was exactly how people would talk, and that's the kind of mood I grew up with."

For me as a therapist, that is an absolute gift. They are giving me the best self-representation that they can find of the emotional climate that shaped them. And I am not having to intuit or guess. I have actually been given it. This is it. So, with my knowledge of movies—because I am a film buff and movies have shaped my life—I am able to empathise more deeply, and follow through what the memory and the experience are about.

One major benefit is that it gets round denial very quickly. If someone is watching the movie from a third-person perspective, they are able to have some objectivity about their feelings.

Peter: Although I have been watching movies since I was very young, my working approach to films was first as a reviewer.

Reviewing has always seemed to me to be the mediating of the movies to people, to audiences. I had to get to know and appreciate my readership well so that I could communicate my experience of the film to them. I have been doing it for a long time now but it is still tricky. For instance, I tend to be rather introverted but I have to review so many 'extroverted' movies. When I began to appreciate this—over twenty years ago—I remember writing that anybody going to see Clint Eastwood, his bare-knuckle fights and his orang-utan Clive, in *Any Which Way But Loose*, needed to remember that it seemed to be made for Extroverts Anonymous.

I also worked for a long time with students in the religious order I belong to, many of whom were also training for priesthood. But I was able to take them with me to film previews and review screenings, and I found that the movies were helping me to understand how the various students ticked. I noted which student would like a particular film—there were two who always booked the Westerns!—or disliked a particular film or could not deal with it. And I was learning this before I had any language to use to name what was happening. It was clear that the film experience was different for different people.

In the late 70s I was introduced to the Jungian approach to Personality Type as developed by the Americans, Katherine Briggs and her daughter, Isabel Myers. They had adopted Jung's categories on Type and how we function. So I found myself looking at movies, especially those that were well-written and which showed a more real understanding of human nature, and seeing that they were dramatising particular types and different ways of functioning.

I found that this was helpful not only with counselling the seminarians but also in working with people in groups. In seminars with school staff, for instance, I show them clips from movies which illustrate how they might function, as being intuitive, say, or as being a sensing type, or which dramatises the way somebody else functions differently from the way they do—a 'let's get on with the show' type, compared with someone who always wants more information before they can decide and act. There are scenes of complementary interactions with which they can identify as individuals or as staff as well as of type conflict. To that extent it is not a therapy exercise but I am sure that it is therapeutic in the sense that people are identifying their own traits from what they see and identify with on the screen. That has become an important part of my approach to movies. But each of us has a specific religious background. Yours is Buddhism?

Bernie: My Buddhism! I would not say that Buddhism has a monopoly—I have no practice or beliefs about that—on spiritual ways to God or God-experience, but that is the way for me. It would probably be best to use the vehicle of a movie like *Awakenings* to make my point.

As a Buddhist I found that, interestingly enough, I was a better Christian! What I find fascinating about Buddhism is that it is not a religion of belief. It is a religion of experience. You have drawn on Carl Jung in your approach. He was very important for me because of the interview he did in the late 1950s with John Freeman. Freeman asked him whether he believed in God. And he said "No"—which shook us all up. And then he said "I know"; and from that moment I realised that what was very deep in me was the conviction that it was possible to know and that it was different. Religion in Western countries is about belief.

But I immersed myself in following Eastern practices and I found the Buddhist way to be the best for me. Just in the observing of the breath. The essence of the observing of the breath is in training the mind to be in the moment. And when you truly realise that you are in the moment, you cannot be obsessing or worrying about the future or the past. Free from all that anxiety, you are purely energised in the moment with a great deal of visual, emotional and physical clarity, which I would say is a glimpse of Enlightenment.

I think *Awakenings* is a classic example for illustrating the very powerful way my Buddhism and my understanding of Buddhism affect me. When the doctors are giving the patients in the New York clinic L-Dopa, and some of them, such as the character Leonard, played by Robert de Niro, are brought out of their handicap (for want of a better word), that is like an awakening in the Buddhist sense. When a Buddhist is meditating, everything drops away, all the conditioning drops away.

It is exactly like that at the moment when Leonard awakes from the prison that he has been kept in with his illness (his condition, a kind of catatonic coma) and he comes right into the present moment. His physical condition drops away. But, because of the experience of being locked in that condition for years and the terrifying sword of Damocles hanging over his head that he may well very soon regress, he has something to tell us.

Peter: It is interesting that from my Catholic background, as a member of a religious order, and as having been a priest for many years, I find that I agree with you that there has been too much emphasis on belief in western Christianity and in the Catholic Church. There is affirmation for those who see themselves as orthodox, who are strong on acknowledging the truth of their faith. But Saint Augustine said that faith in the sense of commitment to God, our experience and faith in action, are equally important. I think that is what we are trying to rediscover in many of the Christian churches in recent decades; so when I look at a film like *Awakenings*, while I appreciate your focus on Enlightenment, I am responding with something of a dialogue between the movie and the gospel.

I chose *Awakenings* for a consideration of the raising of Lazarus from the dead, in *John 11*. Lazarus is always used as an image of Jesus and the resurrection—Jesus' fullness of resurrection—because, in fact, Lazarus is actually resuscitated and he must die again. It is similar to the experience of Leonard, who is raised from a kind of death but soon goes back into his 'prison condition', as you called it. Leonard's awakening in the movie can make us ask what the meaning is of Lazarus coming alive again? What was the experience of death that he had been through? How did that affect how he would live his regained life? He has to face dying again. *Awakenings* is a reminder of our mortality but also of the 'grace' that can bring us to life during our lives: our graced moments.

When you spoke of the breath and of the now, I am reminded of a spiritual writer of the eighteenth century, Jean de Caussaude, who used a phrase that was a feature of our formation years: the 'sacrament of the present moment'. The present moment is a visible, tangible way of being in touch with God. In a sense, that was what Lazarus was brought to: he had died once, he had to die again, but he had the opportunity to live in the now: this sacrament of the present moment.

But how does your Buddhist approach help you to appreciate the character of Dr Sayer, played by Robin Williams, and based on Dr Oliver Sacks with whom Williams spent a lot of time in preparation for the movie? What of Dr Sayer's own journey?

Bernie: In many ways he was very concentrated, but he wasn't concentrated as being a person in the world. He was concentrated on his clients, but he left his self out. He was in the tradition of selfless heroes who leave themselves out of their own lives, like James Stewart's George Bailey in *It's a Wonderful Life*. As he progresses through the movie, it seems to me that his engagement with Leonard brings him to realise what it is to be 'in the moment'. He has to come to terms with, for instance, simply having a coffee with his nurse assistant, instead of automatically saying no, that he was busy and going home to play his piano, instead of burying himself in studying hundreds of different microbes, or in his workaholic devotion to using L-Dopa.

It is as if he is somehow escaping from life, but the down-to-earth nurse and the experience with Leonard brings him out of that. I think that a crucial symbolic moment occurs when Leonard smashes Dr Sayer's glasses but, after a time, he gives back the glasses, mended. It is as if Dr Sayer does not see! And it is a symbol that he does not see! But when he is given back his glasses, he *does* see.

And then there is the sequence in the auditorium when he is speaking to his peers about what all the patients, especially Leonard, have been saying about their experience. It is we who have the problem in our lack of ability to understand.

At the same time it was very interesting that Leonard had for years in his condition been subject to physical control, that is, his paralysed body. But after his awakening, the hospital authorities still enforce their own external physical control over him.

So the scene where the glasses are smashed is the scene where both Leonard and Dr Sayer are each grappling with their individual problems. That is a climax and they are both beginning to make their breakthrough. It is not so much an enlightenment on the part of Dr Sayer but it is an important experiential and spiritual insight of psychological growth.

Peter: I agree with that. However, my angle is determined by my interest in Psychological Type. And I was looking at Dr Sayer as being very introverted. He seems to be an intuitive type, always with his theories—even about L-Dopa and the patients. His decision-making, however, is very objective: he likes to construct objective big pictures, of science that can work. But he is patient and can 'go with the flow'. In Type terms, the letters INTP are used as a description for that kind of character. But the problem with Dr Sayer is that he lives so much in the mind that he is divorced from the reality of the body.

Bernie: That he is not embodied.

Peter: So I see his journey certainly as one of insight (and the symbolism of seeing and not seeing through the glasses). But the sequence which comes to mind is where he went with the patients and they danced—and he could not. When he was invited to participate in the dance with them, he gained some sense of bodily wholeness, a totality of his personality which he lacked, especially because of his shyness. He had initially refused the cup of coffee with his sympahetic nurse but, after the episode you mentioned with the glasses, when all the patients have reverted to their comatose stage, he experiences his awakening, enabled and empowered by what has happened. Concretely then, although he automatically refuses the cup of coffee yet again, he can change his mind. And he 'awakens'. This is where his sacrament of the present moment is on this night. Here and now, to have a cup of coffee with this person who has helped me, who has worked with me, who has a devotion to me and whom I appreciate—this is a way of being in the world concretely.

Bernie: I could not agree with you more. And using your Myers Briggs' language, it is the nurse who supplies what is lacking in him, his opposite, his 'inferior function' of personal and practical warmth, it seems to me.

Again, an intersting symbolic moment occurs between Leonard and Dr Sayer, when Leonard walks into the sea: absolute ecstasy and bliss at being liberated from that physical condition, that prison he has been confined in. But Dr Sayer won't go into the water. His psychological prison becomes much more evident. He is very worried, walking up and down nervously, very much out of his depth. Leonard realises the moment and knows what life is about. Dr Sayer is closed to it.

Throughout Leonard's awakening it is something of an experience, in Buddhist terms, of mindfulness. Mindfulness can be described as being completely aware of the moment, just witnessing that moment and noting the thinking, feeling, sensation—there is no judgement of it. Leonard is mindful, so he is very humble when he is observing what is going on. He then finds he has to catch up and learn. But he comes through all of this very quickly and by very 'skilful means', which is another Buddhist term. He eventually finds a 'right way' and 'right speech' to communicate this to Dr Sayer and the others.

Peter: In terms of Christian spirituality, it is said that 'grace builds on nature'. Dr Sayer also has to find his 'right way'. He is strong in his introverted, intitive and objective type, but if he does not develop and branch out (if he does not have his awakening), he will become trapped in that situation and become 'graceless'. Fortunately he has been offered an opportunity. God intervenes, so to speak, in his life and graces him with a situation, which he himself has contributed to, so that he is actually drawn out of himself by Leonard and the patients.

The challenge for him in spirituality terms is, as St Ignatius Loyola and others have said, in an asceticism of spirituality: to go against oneself *(agere contra)*. In Jung's terms that would be not so much a negative thing as going away from oneself, but moving towards one's opposite. And so as he reached out to

Eleanor, the nurse, to go to have a cup of coffee, he was really profoundly doing an exercise in *agere contra*, going against his natural inclination to be reclusive and retiring. And that was a moment of spiritual growth.

Bernie: In Buddhism it is exactly the same. If you find yourself full of anger then you will be asked to practice being full of the opposite as the only antidote. Because that is what makes the complete whole. Rather than being all one, it is the whole, both. In Jungian terms that would be embracing the shadow.

Our conversation about *Awakenings* has shown me that we watch the same movie but bring our own religious background and experiences to appreciating it. We use different language, but there seems to be a closeness in the spiritualities that we express. This gives solid grounding to the use of movies for therapy and healing.

Peter Malone is a counsellor, who is also an Australian Missionary of the Sacred Heart, and World President of the International Catholic Organisation for Cinema

15 CANCER

INTRODUCTION

I faced a difficult question of balance. On the one hand I wanted to give an honest account of my experience; I also wanted to give anyone recently diagnosed or living with cancer some hope—maybe inspiration and assurance.

But as I was writing, its full horror became clear to me, and I was anxious about its possible impact on people facing cancer. I did not want to make it too bleak; but it was. So I have endeavoured to show how I survived: what helped, and what didn't. My intention is to give people some kind of psychological map of what to expect and of what may help.

We all have different strengths and weaknesses. Things that I found hard, you may not, and vice versa. I also hoped it would help any families caring for someone with cancer, and any psychotherapists supporting a client through the journey.

'THERE'S SOMETHING NOT RIGHT'

I had for a few weeks been experiencing bouts of constipation, which was very unusual for me. The climax came while I was on holiday in Bournemouth: the discomfort, together with the symptoms, were disturbing. My doctor referred me to Barnet Hospital for investigations, which would identify any further tests which would be needed.

My wife and I were sitting in the waiting room to see the consultant. He was Korean, a very nice man. He said immediately, "Take your trousers down, lie there on your left side with your knees up to your chest. I'm going to take a biopsy."

I was anxious, but at the same time I had humorous thoughts going through my mind. The whole thing was surreal: I was lying half naked with a complete stranger looking intently up my behind. My mind said, as if it were the doctor speaking to me at that point, "You are going to meet a tall dark stranger." I was quickly distracted from these thoughts when the doctor picked up an unfriendly-looking instrument for the examination. Then to my amazement he said, in broken English, "Open your mouth." My mind raced. Maybe he was confused with the language; or maybe in his culture any orifice could be called a mouth.

All this was soon shockingly dispelled: a searing pain shot through my behind as the doctor plunged the instrument far enough in to take the biopsy.

"Can you keep still?" I looked at him in disbelief, as at that moment I felt all my hair was standing up, like in Tom and Jerry cartoons, when they are really hurt. He sighed and said, "No, it's hurting too much. You'll have to come into surgery for the biopsy."

About a week later I was admitted, the biopsy was taken, and some forty-eight hours later I was back home.

THE DIAGNOSIS

The surgical consultant who saw me was Dr Mitchell.

"Mr Wooder, I'm sorry to say you have a tumour in your bowel, and we must act quickly."

My wife Joy gasped, "Oh, Bern," and her lower lip beginning to tremble. I found myself observing all this in a quiet, dreamlike state, but moved by Joy's obvious deep love for me. We were both in shock.

The doctor explained that treatment would start with six weeks of daily chemotherapy and radiotherapy. He said this was necessary to shrink the tumour prior to the operation. I coped pretty well with the therapies as an outpatient—now at Mount Vernon Hospital, which was some distant from our home in Elstree. As I was told not to drive after the treatment, the problem of getting there and back was resolved by a friend, Anne Page, who organised a rota of friends to ferry me to and from the hospital. I was particularly grateful to Karen Abrams and Hugh Jones, who were the core of this rota; and this gratitude remains with me. The whole experience was humbling, and brought about a re-evaluation of what was important in life.

It was difficult but nessecary to tell my clients I had cancer and see how each one wanted to deal with that fact. I explained that, if they wanted to find another therapist, I would help them. To my great surprise, all seventeen said they would wait for me to get better and come back. This was a very humbling experience for me. So when I returned to working with them after my illness, I had to make it very clear and quite sternly, that they must resist any attempt to look after me and if they felt, they felt compelled to try and look after me, then I would not be able to see them, because that is not therapy.

I was there as their therapist to look after them. They all understood and did not protect me, and some attacked me when necessary with great gusto.

Something I had not considered, that was very therapeutic for my clients, and which they each told me in their own way, was that I was actually modelling how to come through a crisis. They were seeing me walk the walk and talk the talk, as they put it. As some said, it was not coming from books. Others said it made it so real but was reassuring to them.

THE OPERATION AND AFTER

I woke from the operation in intensive care, with a breathing tube in my mouth. The nurse removed it, and she and my family all asked how I felt. I said I'd rather be in Devon, and they laughed. I learned that the three-hour operation had in fact taken eight hours because of complications, in which the ureta had been accidentally cut, and a specialist surgeon had been called in. I'd been given nearly four pints of blood.

I was impressed, yet disturbed, by my wife telling me that the consultant had rung her mobile to say the operation was over and he had cut out all the cancer. She had been travelling by bus to the hospital, and I was impressed because his action was, I thought, unusual; yet disturbed too, because I wondered if he was relieved that I'd survived the operation!

When he examined me during the next day's ward round, looking very tired after the long operation, he said "You look better than I feel!"

Then he went on to say, "I'm sorry, but the region we had to operate on was where your sexual function and your urinary tract are. Sadly, the operation will leave you sexually impotent and requiring a permanent catheter."

"Will it ever go back to functioning healthily?" I asked. He shook his head and said, "No. I don't think so."

The impotence had a huge impact on me, and so the psychological adjustment took a number of years. I no longer knew who I was, or even how to be. The operation had also left me with an inability to pee without a catheter, which I have to use some twelve times a day.

That in itself has required a gradual adjustment: when I'm out socially, I have to check first that the toilet is clean enough to allow me to do what amounts to a medical procedure. I am after all inserting a foot-long catheter into my bladder, and so have to be extremely careful to avoid infection. Furthermore, when I'm asleep, the only warning that I need to pee is racking pains as the stomach muscles go into agonising spasms.

Horror has many aspects: pain, fear, despair, the sounds of suffering, and the never-forgotten smells; feeling permanently sick, hot, dizzy; my mind unable to function during the weird moods and the morphine.

The heartbreaking look in the eyes of my Joy, and also my son and daughter, filled me with guilt for bringing so much suffering on them. The slow dragging days of this surreal nightmare: the man dying a few beds away from me; and Joy visits me, only to be met by my projectile vomiting—green and disgusting, some fifteen bowls of it. All this surely burned into my heart the important things in life.

When Billy, a young American from the deep South, in the bed opposite me, could take no more of his cancer-ridden body, he cried out in anguish and sobbed for hours, on and off, all through that day. His so-loyal and supportive wife implored him to believe his colostomy bag didn't affect her love for him one bit, until he was able gradually to let it in. It was an incident of horror, but also of pure devotion. It also reflected the devotion of Joy, my son and daughter to me.

It was a rape of mind and body that left me with all the symptoms of post-traumatic stress: funny, that they never link it to operations: why?

Gradually things started to get better. I remember one day when my son Jamie was visiting me. He is so matter-of-fact about his own psychic abilities. He just said, "Mum has entered the building." My ward was on the third floor, and I thought, how could he know? A few minutes later, in walked my Joy, all warm smiles and grapes. Amazing, I thought; but Jamie himself thought nothing of it.

After a month in the hospital, I was sent home. Disappointingly, after three days I had to be readmitted. One evening I was feeling depressed and very low, and I rang my home. My daughter Claire answered, and listened quietly as I told her how unbearable it all was. She just gave me the perfect answer: "Nothing's permanent, dad." That buddhist answer, that I'd taught her over many years, came back to help me in that moment: so much so that I'll never forget my daughter's wisdom.

PAINFUL ADJUSTMENTS

Learning how to use the stoma bag was a horrible and shaming experience; and it was hard to adjust to the sight of the ugly open wound across my stomach, together with two large disfiguring hernias, with which I would now have to live for ever.

The hospital policy required that I look at the wound—a sight that filled me with revulsion and sadness, and the realisation that I was no longer like other people. The toilet had now been replaced by the bag. This meant a complete loss of control—I no longer decided when to go to the toilet: it was decided for me by the bag. It was a process that I have to say produced sounds and smells that of course caused acute embarrassment. Imagine: it was akin to inviting any and everyone I was with to join me in the toilet.

A nurse told me I would not be able to go home until I could take complete responsibility for the procedure—removing and replacing the bag and meticulously washing the wound.

Apart from feeling like a social pariah, or a pathetic leper, the loss of my sexual functioning was another terrible journey through loss and isolation. The doctors tried in vain with various prescriptions—Viagra, and something called a pump which I can only think must be a relic of the Spanish Inquisition.

How anyone could expect one to go through that process before making love, not to mention its effect on your wife's desire, was beyond me. The frustration of continued sexual feelings, but an inability to act on them, produced in me periods of deep depression and sadness. The rage inside me was enormous; and the questions that tormented me were: Who was I? What was I? and Why me? My own answer to the last was: Why not?

THE CRUEL FRIEND

After the final operation to reposition the bag to a lower, more comfortable and practical position, people came to visit me once I was sent home.

A friend came one day with his wife. At that time I was feeling particularly broken. For some unconcious reason, he felt compelled to tell me, "You're an old man." Later he said it again. I felt a rage building inside me. He was kicking me when I was down. How could he do that? Fortunately his wife was apalled and took him to task. How would he like to be called an old man? Suitably chastised, he shut up. He is, ironically enough, some five years older than I. It is something I will never forget. Strange.

THE STITCHES BURST

I'd been home a few days, but didn't feel good. I had developed a cough, and a visiting good friend—a nurse, Viv Eldridge— insisted we immediately call an ambulance. We did, although I dreaded going back to hospital. Waiting in Accident and Emergency, I started coughing again. I suddenly felt something wet running down my tummy and legs. Frightened to look, I reached down with my hands and to my horror saw blood everywhere. My stitches had burst.

I was in shock, and for a moment I didn't know if my intestines would fall out. It was a living nightmare. I was admitted immediately for another eight days.

Back home again, one day I was deeply depressed. It was so heavy it felt as if my eyelashes were laced with lead.

I thought about trying ease it in a Buddhist way—just feel the depression, be open to it. Easier said than done, I found: every cell and and instinct in me strained for distraction. I decided to lie on the floor to attempt this. My mind offered distractions—have a cup of tea, go out, have an alcoholic drink—but I stayed with it, while the thoughts, the yearning for distraction, came in waves. It was a titanic struggle.

I started to cry out, and the sound shook me: it was like a wounded animal. Hearing the anguish in my cry brought huge uncontrollable sobs, each of which seemed too big for me. I couldn't get my breath; hearing the sound of my suffering only increased the hurt. I sounded like an alien, I felt like an alien; this was a part of me I never knew existed. It all built up to unbearable intensity. Then suddenly all the hurt and depression was gone and I was flooded with a tsunami of healing, of love through my whole body. It melted the pain, the despair, the depression so easily, until there wasn't a vestige of it anywhere. The image that came to me was symbolic: the wave of love was the white cliffs of Dover, the suffering was now the smallest pebble on the beach, the towering cliffs dwarfed the suffering, I realised in that moment that nothing can beat love and compassion.

The most important revelation that came to me as I lay there was that it's not the heart that breaks but the defensive crust around it. Once you get to the heart it is invincible: there is nothing bigger, and nothing can defeat it.

My feelings about my bag, about my disfigured body, were gone, I was OK, and all was right with the world. I felt complete, whole, in fact more safe and whole that I had ever felt in my life; no shame, only softness; no embarrassment, only this inner softness; no longer any feelings, ravaged rawness, I just felt healed psychologically and emotionally.

The impact was noticeable in my demeanour and mood. Buoyed up by this meeting with my heart, I tried to achieve the same thing whenever the depression came, and through some eight attempts I succeeded in achieving it three times. But the first experience had left me with confidence and the knowledge that my suffering wasn't infallible, and by grace I could experience my heart's momentous healing power again.

In one attempt just to lie there and feel the depressing shame, I had the most unusual experience of what I can only describe as a vision. Now, it's important to assert that I'm a very down to earth man; but suddenly I looked up and saw around me what I can only describe as huge beings, each one pure white. I could see none of their faces, but somehow I knew they were all peering down at me in a benevolent way, as if I were lying in the centre of the flower and the beings were the petals. I heard one say, "He thinks he's suffering". My immediate, angry response was, "I *am* suffering!" But something happened: somehow those four words started to expand space around my suffering. I was physically less contracted; it changed my perspective so that everything became more bearable. My relationship to my suffering had changed.

I developed a discipline of consciously remembering the better days, when I felt good and happy moments, when I was the same as everyone else and no longer isolated. I practiced this relentlessly until it became a conditioned reflex, so when I was down or facing more pain, all the good days and things would just come into consciousness after the conditioned reflex.

THE DREAM THAT HEALED

Anyone who has back pain knows its agony. As I mentioned earlier, my back pain was activated after I stopped taking the tramadol and was due an epidural injection for my back. Then I had the most amazing dream: I was on an old galleon which was struggling in heavy seas; huge waves crashed over the deck, and the storm raged stronger and stronger.

Suddenly I was on the beach, looking out to sea. In front of me was a huge giant, the water coming up to his ankles and his head touching the clouds; he was a cheery oriental man and he came strolling towards me, holding in his left hand an old fashioned milkmaid's pail, made of wood with a wide rim at the top, and with a thick rope handle. When I looked inside the bucket, I saw to my astonishment that it contained the ocean, the storm, and the huge galleon on which I had been stranded. They were all inside the bucket. I was awestruck.

I woke the next day and was astounded: the pain in my back had gone. I could not believ it: all those months of agony had vanished overnight. I waited a few days before telling everybody that the pain, which had been a constant companion, was now gone. I didn't analyse it, I was just immensely grateful it had gone, leaving just another unforgettable memory. This was to me nothing short of miraculous.

HUMOUR

The humour I had always used was another factor—like the day I bought home nine boxes of tissues and forgot to put them away, so they were still on the sofa when an early client arrived who had to catch a plane straight after seeing me.

He was Jewish and as he came in, he saw the stack of tissues and said "Business must be good!", opening his hands as he said it to emphasise his Jewishness. I really laughed when writing this. I contacted him for his permission to tell this funny incident. He was enthusiastic and said, "Of course! I'm proud of my therapy! Make it like I'm the good Jewish boy I am." He had finished therapy years earlier, and it was a nice reconnection.

Another funny incident: a client had left his shoes in the hall by the door when the session was finished. He put on his shoes and left. Next session he told me his wife had said, "I haven't seen those shoes before." He didn't think much of it, but I remembered my son, who was living with us at the time, saying his shoes were a bit tight. The penny dropped: my client had been wearing my son's shoes for a week, and of course my son had been wearing his. This produced disbelief, laughter and incredulity; but clearly they both walk much more comfortably now. I'm sure that memory will come back to them when buying shoes at Marks and Spencers.

PSYCHOLOGICAL AND EMOTIONAL RECOVERY

Gradually I started feeling better, as the idea and practice of remembering the good days momentarily helped with the despairing days. My psychotherapy practice was continuing to go well; and in addition, the positive aspect of what I was going through was that my heart had been so opened that my compassion and empathy for my clients was increased, and its effect on my clients was to deepen the relationship and their disclosure. I had told them all that they must not adopt a role of looking after me, and if they did, I could no longer see them as that would obstruct the therapy. They kept firmly to what I had said, as will become evident in the case study "Mac".

Meanwhile I got more interviews on radio and television, which furthered my sense of achievement. My clients felt in their own ways that I was providing them with a valuable model for working through a crisis. This I had not expected, but each of them put that to me in their own way. This, combined with my growing knowledge of the right foods, considerably reduced any embarrassment or shame from the grumbling bag. The shared joy of clients making important breakthroughs and having life-changing insights, deepened the sense of meaning for my life.

My level of appreciation has increased considerably and I feel reborn, and grateful for all I have, especially my family, including now my adorable granddaughter Amber. I am increasingly aware of how rich I am in emotional terms—a thought which always brings to mind the last scene of the film *It's a Wonderful Life*, where they're all standing by a Christmas tree and George Bailey's brother is making a speech. He turns to George and says, "And my brother is a millionaire". The significance is that George is bankrupt; but his community comes together to make a donation and put him back on his feet. So George feels that he is emotionally a millionaire.

That scene so speaks to me and brings tears of inner contentment with all I have: my lovely wife Joy, who has a permanent look of amazement, huge green eyes, and who is very funny but completely unaware of it. Our heart to heart relationship is a continuous transmission of healing for me. We have been married 43 years and I would marry her again tomorrow.

My daughter Claire is insightful, kind and emotionally intelligent. Her gift is her ability to analyse a complex issue, simplify it and communicate its essentials. Her competence on the computer on behalf of her dad is a wonderful support.

My son Jamie has some of Joy's permanent amazement. His kindness and deep spirituality are often capable of giving me healing insights. I am a very lucky man and feel much loved.

All this, plus my practice, feels me with a sense of richness and meaning. As I write this the sun is shining and the world and people seem full of vibrant energy. I am now just so aware of the aliveness.

As suffering sensitises you to pain, so joy is also sensitised and increased. Now when I am down, I have made it a discipline to remember when I was up. It works: balance, the middle way, as Bhudda said.

16 FRIENDS: MY INFORMAL SANGHA?

Viv and Pete Eldridge are very good friends. Viv is a ward sister: the consummate professional. She is also wonderfully scatty, unconsciously funny, and a force of nature. She is indefatigable—someone who always finds the energy to do more. She has a relentlessly enquiring mind, with a particularly scientific and secular bent. Her musical choice is Meat Loaf.

Her husband Pete is highly intelligent, sensitive and witty. The Rolling Stones have been the soundtrack of his life, and as a natural archivist he has a collection of Stones press cuttings in dated order from the early years of their career. (When he is not being a company secretary he is a drummer; he refers to his ginger hair as Titian—spoken with false pomp as a subtle self mocking.) If he goes on a cruise or other holiday, Pete keeps the tickets and any other memorabilia.

His character, like Rimmer from *Red Dwarf*, is in sharp comical relief to Viv's impulsive sponteneity; he is often in a state of disassociated shock. As Viv tells us of her latest escapade or purchase, of which Pete is completely unaware, he sits there wide-eyed and worried: it is very funny to watch, especially as Viv is oblivious to Pete's horror; or if she is, just dismisses it with a wave of her hand. It could seem sad, but for the fact that Pete knows deep down that Viv will protect them and bulldoze them both through anything. An example of Viv's compulsiveness from some time ago: Pete came home from work to find he had a complete new front room, filled with new furniture, and a new flatpack kitchen waiting for him to install.

Their qualities of compassion and generous giving of themselves are the same qualities central to Buddhism. They represent the quality of Karuna.

Karen and Ian Abrams are great friends, with both of whom you just feel looked after. Karen is a combination of emotional warmth, cool analysis, and wit. She quietly goes about doing good things for people—most importantly for me, driving me to chemo- and radio-therapy at Mount Vernon hospital, Northwood, at least three times a week over a period of some six weeks.

Ian is sincere, quick in thought and movement, naturally courteous and respectful. The world could do with more Ians. He is good at relating stories—the best are usually about Karen—and he has a sharply incisive intelligence. And he drives at a wonderfully comfortable speed.

Ian told us a story about Karen, and the time they took their young children to Florida. In the evening of a long hot day, the kids were disappointed at not having Donald Duck's autograph, and nothing would pacify them. Finally an exasperated Karen ordered Ian to "find Donald Duck!" Ian said "Ok," but in absolute bewilderment at where to start. He told us he had asked several people, until he felt the embarrassment and absurdity of the quest. Finally he signed 'Donald Duck' himself, and it wasn't discovered by his sons until seventeen years later. Both Ian and Karen had the quality of sympathetic joy in other people's good fortune—*muditta*, in Buddhism—and compassion—*karuna.*

Hugh Jones was a lecturer, his wife Pat a deputy headmistress. Hugh helped me through my treatment by taking me to Mount Vernon hospital when Karen couldn't do it, sometimes four days in a week. Hugh is, under his cool scientific exterior, a passionate man, a committed atheist who knows the Bible better than most Christians—but in his actions he is dependable and supportive. Pat is strikingly good looking, very sophisticated, every inch the Haberdashers Aske educated woman. She is down to earth—a brilliant mimic, who reads voraciously. Hugh has a wonderful childlike quality when he is showing you one of his latest gizmos; when Pat watches him at these moments her love for him is beautiful to see.

Anne Page is the person who swiftly organised my hospital rota to Mount Vernon. She is very practical, an excellent cook and host, and we have enjoyed our invitations to dinner at Anne's home over many years. She has a very distinctive soft voice, is a committed socialist and has a gift for maps and directions. She is investigative and analytical in conversation, very practical and kind, loves *The Archers*; she is spiritual and had an unusual yoga guru—unusual in that he was an ex miner! Anne is also a natural nurse, and a good exponent on the Middle Way.

Some months after, when I was able to drive myself to Mount Vernon, a funny incident occurred. A policeman waved me down to pull over, and said, in a very policeman-like manner, "We're not a member of the Wide-Awake Club this morning, are we, sir?" I was momentarily confused, till it dawned on me that he was looking at my unclipped seatbelt. I apologised in the manner of Uriah Heep: "I'm sorry officer. I'm just on my way to Mount Vernon for more cancer tests." At which he changed magically from policeman into kindness iself, and waved me on with a "Good luck, sir". I saw a completely different side to him.

Another close, if new, friend is Brian. He is a kind sincere man. His sense of care makes you feel very comfortable. He is a dynamic man, who's had a thirty-year career as a camera man for films and television. He is also a film script writer, author and businessman. In fact, you get with Brian the sense that he could do anything he set his mind to.

He shows much compassion in his listening, and his intelligence is intellectual and emotional. I enjoy his company, and our joint interest in films, biographies and humour always makes our meetings interesting and fun. Brian is sixty-eight, and exudes a very strong life force, which becomes especially bright when he talks about his grandchildren.

Alicia Drewnowska was my Polish psychotherapist—the best therapist I ever had. It was so timely that I met her during the period around my cancer diagnosis in 2004: she helped me tremendously, and still now in 2011 I cannot fully express how much. I have no doubts about the efficacy of good psychotherapists, but when she had to leave for Poland it felt like the cruellest blow, as if the gods were playing with me.

Milton and Elinor Simanowitz are two South Africans who have been very supportive friends. Milton, until recently a leading gynaecologist, has retired to become a trained teacher of the Alexander method. He is also studying French, and is a painter. He did in fact paint a good portrait likeness of me. In appearance he is not unlike a young Laurens van der Post. He can be alternatively friendly and stern; he is interested in politics and world events, and we have many interesting and sometimes comical conversations. Spiritually I feel he would like to find a path, but nothing has so far stood up to his critical anaysis of what they offer. My sense is that his spiritual life is in the place he enters when he paints.

Elinor was for many years a family social worker, and is now a psychoanalytical psychotherapist, trained at the Lincoln. She is very intelligent and intuitive, which is often hidden by a spaced-out quality: now you see her, now you don't, as when you glimpse the sun through trees. There is a private part of her which is always sifting and observing: she is there for you, and yet deep and distant. She is wonderfully absent-minded, and many funny things happen to and around Elinor. In such situations Milton looks on with loving bemusement. They too manifest important Buddhist qualities of *upeka* (equanimity) and *karuna* (compassion).

Chris Sheedy, who sadly is no longer with us, was a rock of compassion, humility, moral values and strength. This huge Irishman—ex heavyweight wrestling champion of Ireland—was a very good friend to me. He was politically astute, and we spent many an hour over a pint, discussing everything under the sun from politics to religion, including his beloved Arsenal. He had that wonderful Irish gift of telling stories accompanied by a twinkle of humour in his eye. He went to see his last Arsenal game and died on the underground on his way home. I miss him.

Chris always showed his wife, Tess, a respect that was moving. Tess matched him in presence, but was not active like Chris, so I did not meet her often; but it was clear she was the woman behind him, enabling him to do all that he did for others. She had a quiet dignity, and would often tease Chris and smile when she managed to bemuse him.

17 TRIP TO AMERICA

On holiday in the United States, I was looking forward to a guided tour of the prison island of Alcatraz, in the Bay of San Francisco. There was a choice of two boat trips, but I booked the wrong one. I'd meant to take the boat that docked on the island and included a guided tour on foot of the prison; instead we just circled the island in the boat, while the guide gave a commentary of Alcatraz's history and some of its more notorious inmates.

Disappointed, I went looking for the best book on the prison that I could find. I asked one of the bookstore staff and was directed to the far corner. I walked over and started browsing.

All of a sudden a deep, cultured American voice asked, "Can I help you, sir?" I turned to see a huge man with blond and grey hair. He was very well built, but pain showed in his face.

"Oh," I said, "I missed the guided tour of Alcatraz, so I just wanted a good book on it."

He smiled and asked, "What do you want to know? I spent ten years on the rock as a prisoner." I was, to put it mildly, stunned. He smiled again at my surprise, while I tried desperately to come up with a question good enough for this unmissable opportunity.

"How did you cope with the fear each day," I asked, "being in a prison with some of the most dangerous prisoners in the world?"

"Sir," he said politely, "you don't understand. When you don't care if you live or die, you have no fear." What an answer, I thought. He was a man of great dignity, and the authority of his experience was impressive.

"Could you say more?" I asked. "About yourself, your experiences, who you met in there?"

"Well, my name is Leon 'Whitey' Thompson, and I'm from Swedish parents who came to America. We were very poor farmers. I was young and strong and got into trouble with the law. So I started a life of crime and prison. But I was also very good at escaping from prison, and because I got a reputation for escaping, they finally sent me to Alcatraz. I was there for ten years and released when they closed it down."

"Who was in there at that time?"

"Oh, Al Capone. Robert Stroud—the Birdman of Alcatraz. Frank Lee Morris—a man with a genius IQ of 159, who subsequently escaped with his two brothers who worked in the tailors' shop. Richard Morris got them to make three ordinary-looking suits, but to make them so they were inflatable."

"Were they successful?" I asked.

"Well, the authorities said they must have drowned, but they never found the bodies. What do you think?" He smiled broadly. "And I think they got away; because you're not going to pose for your picture on the front of *Time*, are you?"

"What about Al Capone?"

"Oh," he said with a contemptuous look, "he was scared

stiff. That's why he wanted to stay in the prison hospital. He had a lot of enemies."

He continued: "The birdman, Robert Stroud, was absolutely brilliant with birds. Mice as well. He could fix them even if they looked half dead. He was so gentle with animals. But he hated people. He was in for murder; he even murdered two of the prison guards."

I was listening, fascinated and spellbound, to this oral history. Leon then told me he had written a book on it—though I felt he had no great interest in persuading me to buy it. His initial reason for talking to me was the fact that I was English and he liked the Cockney accent. At any rate, I asked him how he had come to write his book.

"Well," he said, "I would never accept letters or visitors."

"Why?" I asked.

"Well," he explained, "then the guards had nothing to punish you with. I'd taken away my own privileges. They told me some woman kept writing to me, wanting to be a penpal. After a long time I accepted her letters; we wrote to each other for years, and we became close.

"When I came out, there she was with a car, and so English! I was amazed—that this blue-rinse middle-aged woman from Orpington, England, would be a penpal to a prisoner of Alcatraz. But she was the making of me. She told me, 'Leon, you have to write a book'."

He told her he'd tried, but couldn't do it. Undeterred, she had hired a ghost writer, but fired him because, she said, he was taking away Leon's character, his voice. Still determined, she ordered Leon one day: "Sit down and tell me your story from the beginning." She switched on the tape recorder and told him, "This is how we'll do it: you speak, and I'll type up the transcript."

That was how they did it, and I was very impressed. In fact, I did exactly the same when I wrote my first book, and much of this one.

We had been talking for some time, and I asked Leon what he was doing now. He gave a broad smile and said, "I'm poacher turned gamekeeper. I work for the government educational programme." Chuckling, he explained, "I go round talking to teenagers at high schools and colleges, and tell them what it's really like in prison. The idea is to make them realise it's not glamorous like in the films. It's a lot of suffering."

I smiled inwardly at the irony and wisdom of what he was now doing. We shook hands, and of course I had to buy his book, *Rock Hard*. He signed it for me and we said goodbye.

I feel lucky to have met him, and in fact for the whole experience: understanding how this man, who must have been seventy-five, had turned his life around in spite of all his suffering.

18 THE HEALING POWER OF MOVIES

Extract from David (Lord) Puttnam's BAFTA Fellowship Acceptance Speech at the Orange British Academy Film Awards, 19 February 2006

114 Just a couple of weeks before I won the BAFTA award for *Chariots of Fire* and then went on and won it in Los Angeles, won the Oscar, my Dad had died. And so this charismatic, this extraordinary man and I never had the opportunity to exchange that glance or hug each other. And that left a hole. But movies you know have got an amazing way of detecting those moments. They speak to us. Every single one of you has sat in a movie house and watched some moment of your life healed, or addressed, or touched. Something that you thought that only you knew. There are a number of films I could relate that did this but I've only got time for one.

Bear with me.

I guess a lot of you, I hope a lot of you, saw the movie *The Sixth Sense*. It's a very fine film. Do you remember the final scene when Toni Collette is in the car with her son? She's had a very difficult life, she's a single mother who's had a tough time, and she's had to come to terms with the fact that her son can speak to the spirit world. And the little boy says to her "Mummy, is it true, Grandma told me that shortly after she died you went and visited her graveside?"

And Toni Collette says "Yeah, that's true."

"And Grandma said you asked her a question. Is that true?"

She says, "Yeah. Yes, I did ask Grandma a question."

"Well," he says, "Grandma wants you to know that the answer to that question is 'Yes, every single day.' But Mum, what was the question?"

Toni Collette starts to cry and through her tears she says "I just asked her if she'd ever been proud of me."

I remember that hitting me like a punch in the stomach. And tonight I know absolutely for sure I never really have to ask the question again; but thanks to you and your generosity my Dad's very proud, my family's very proud and I am more proud than I ever believed I could be.

Thank you so much.

The author is grateful to Lord Puttnam for his permission to reproduce this extract from his speech.

19 INTRODUCING MAC

What follows are prime moments from a fascinating case study where film has been of major therapeutic benefit to my client.

The phone rang one evening. "Is that Bernie Wooder?" the caller asked in a soft Scottish accent.

"Yes it is," I replied.

"My name is Mac and I've been in therapy with Steve. We are ending our sessions as he is moving to Spain. He gave me your telephone number as a therapist he could recommend, so I am wondering, do you have spaces to see me?"

"I'll just get my diary. I have a space at 7pm on Tuesday evenings. Could you make that?"

"Yes, that's fine," he said.

I gave him my address and explained that it would be an exploratory session to see if we could work together. He agreed.

As I replaced the receiver I felt his discomfort through the phone. It was quite cleverly concealed, but I felt there was something I couldn't quite put my finger on. Our work had started.

The following evening I came home from my clinic in Golders Green to find an envelope on my mat. It had been delivered by hand by Mac, although he lived some distance away. To my surprise it contained a quite detailed history of Mac's life and his current preoccupations about coming to see me, or continuing with therapy at all.

I found it very interesting that someone would drive twenty miles to deliver something like that the day after a phone call to meet; and wondered why. There was a kind of urgency with this situation, but at the same time ambivalence on Mac's part about coming at all. I began to realise it was going to be very interesting working with him.

The following day was Mac's appointment. He stood about 6ft tall. His energy was wary, his face somehow held back, chin in, eyes quickly surveying me, a slight smile, hand extended.

"Hello Bernie," he said in his soft Scottish burr.

"Hello Mac. Come in."

In the session room Mac took off his polished brown leather shoes, placing them at an angle to his left, then put his wallet and car keys in the shoe nearest to him. As he went through this methodical routine, he seemed somehow in a world of his own, totally absorbed, as if I wasn't there. This turned out to be the ritual of order that Mac would go through at the beginning of every session.

I began. "This is a getting to know each other session for you to see how you feel with me." I then asked him how it felt leaving Steve, his previous therapist.

"Oh, you know, sad." He seemed nervous, uncomfortable, just looking at me as if to say 'Help me out here'. Bearing in mind the amount of information about himself Mac had sent me, I was trying to gauge a comfortable pace of one-to-one disclosure for him.

"How does it feel meeting me?"

"It feels strange, a bit disorientating really," he said, smiling and looking a bit more comfortable.

"Yes, it must do. How long did it take you to end?" I asked, referring to ending therapy with Steve.

"About four weeks."

"Did you feel that was long enough?"

"Yeah, it was OK."

"OK, really? I wonder if you have some other feelings that are not OK?"

Mac waited for a while and sighed.

"I think I am sad and angry at the same time. After all, my close relationship with Steve has ended. How can I ever find anyone or anything else to replace that?"

Inside I felt that this was better, more real. It gave me a clearer understanding of what therapy with Steve had meant to Mac. A kind of longing and despair in the question "How can I find anyone to replace Steve?' seemed to denote this.

After a pause Mac said, "Perhaps that's why there's a lump in my throat at present. It's been around on and off, ever since Tuesday evening, which would normally have been the time I spent discussing my issues with Steve." Mac looked directly in my eyes. "Just to make things interesting, I am now seeing you, Bernie, on Tuesday evenings at this time. Yet another yardstick to measure things by."

I was astounded. Somehow I had unknowingly managed to make the same time on the same day for our sessions that Mac had arranged with his previous therapist.

He continued, "I'm pissed off because my comfortable

routine has been disrupted. Also I am feeling the terrible onset of deep seated anxiety."

"What are you anxious about?"

Mac paused. "If I'm going to make a go of this, I'm going to be open with you about what I am feeling. It raises many questions in me."

"What kind of questions?"

"Well, why do I want to see a therapist? This question has got me vexed for the moment. I've scrambled around for reasons, ideas, thoughts—possibly trying to justify my actions to myself. Seems to be a common theme in my life, this self-doubt."

His face clouded over with anxiety. "Self-doubt, anxiety and apprehension are not uncommon feelings and I'm not alone in experiencing them but something doesn't feel healthy." He moved around restlessly and sighed.

"Mac, I'm feeling a little confused. What is the something that does not feel healthy?"

Mac replied somewhat testily, "The circumstances of my childhood; the atmosphere; the lack of guidance and support. All served as bloody good reasons not to trust or show any part of my emotional self to anyone."

"How does that make you feel?"

"Cut off from people and from myself," he said despairingly. Then he got quite angry. "Here I am contemplating revealing myself to someone I know next to nothing about. Fuck. Even if you, Bernie, do know Steve and Steve knows you, what does that mean? That I'll feel we can work together? Or even that you can work with me? I am busy torturing myself with this idea."

"I'm a bit confused Mac. Which idea?"

Mac completely disregarded my question and continued.

"Already I'm trying to gauge you, yet I have absolutely nothing to go on. Dick all. Zilch. Zero. In my mind I'm wondering how you will measure up against my experience with Steve. After all I did spend two years and seven months seeing him on a once a week basis. I know I covered a lot of ground with him: not plain sailing but beneficial nevertheless." He was moving from side to side in the armchair, fists clenched unconciously and at times stuttering slightly.

I glanced at the clock. We were just about two minutes until the end, not enough time to address any of the questions lining up in my mind.

"Well, we'll just have to take it gradually to see if you feel you can work with me and to see if I feel I can work with you. But I must say, Mac, I have no reservations on my side. We have about two minutes to go before we end and I don't want to raise anymore questions at present."

Mac glanced up, smiled, looked relieved and started to put his shoes on.

MAC'S HISTORY

Mac arrived and again, as I opened the door, his face subtly moved back as if he were waiting for a problem. I noted this subtle facial and bodily movement. "Come in Mac."

Mac sat down, surveying the room as he leaned back in the chair. This survey of the room was total. He took in every object, ensuring that the door was closed. He checked the windows and even checked me out, looking deeply into my eyes and remaining silent for a while. I felt like I was in the presence of someone who had been in the Special Air Service (SAS).

I asked myself what this man was trying to establish. Then after a moment the answer just popped into my head. It seemed so obvious—it was safety—he was checking his surroundings in every session to ensure that he was safe. This explained why he was the only client to bring his shoes into the session room. He needed to have his shoes with him in case he had to run.

"Can you tell me about your childhood Mac?" Mac's right hand became a fist.

"My childhood was miserable," he said in a grey voice. "I'm becoming more and more aware of its full horror. Memories come back to me of my father beating my mother up. There was a regular cycle of mother leaving, taking myself and my sister to stay with a maternal Gran when things went too far. She always ended up going back, saying things would be different this time. I lost count of the number of times this pattern repeated itself. Five times possibly. I don't know and tried not to care."

This was a disturbing story already. The tone of Mac's voice, the involuntary jumps of his body as he talked and the fact that it was a dark winter night outside, with the trees throwing shadows on my garden, only added to the cold, hatred-filled atmosphere developing in the room.

"My father was violent, threatening, terrifying—an unpredictable bully with a short fuse. He only ever targeted my mother with his physical and verbal abuse and made sure he destroyed and damaged her possessions when in one of his deranged moods."

Mac went very quiet. I just sat there, letting him have his space to think and remember but not feel pressured in any way.

Mac continued, "It has taken me a long time to realise his behaviour was not normal and that he was mentally unbalanced during these times." Then, as an afterthought, he said, "Not that I could relate to his behaviour prior to or post these periods. I think he used alcohol to deaden his inner pain, a pain that was often unleashed upon my family with disastrous consequences for my mum."

Mac's knuckles went white as he clenched his fists unconsciously. The atmosphere in the room became even more tense while all this poured out of him.

He looked incredibly angry now and his voice rose. "Fuck. How I hated and despised him. My father was a monster whom I somehow felt totally ashamed of and responsible for—one who scared the living daylights out of me. It was like living on the slopes of a volcano about to erupt. I was, and I still am, fearful of the memory I hold of him."

Mac went quiet, his breathing very laboured. "My father joined the army when he was young. He was in the Royal Scots Parades as a piper for 10 years plus. From what I know he carried on with other women even when he was going out with my mum and was violent towards her from the start. Why do I think that?" he questioned himself. "Why did my mum stay with him?" The questions kept coming. "What did she see in him? I feel angry and resentful towards her for this."

As I sat there listening, the chaotic childhood that Mac was describing reverberated through me emotionally and mentally. I noticed my own hands were clenched into fists.

Then Mac, his face softer now, said surprisingly, "I would like to know more about his life in the army as a piper—to feel proud of him—but all that is too late now. All I can remember in my childhood was the actual violence or the impending threat of it."

"Mac, how did you cope with all this?"

He looked at me and sighed. He had coped, he explained, by withdrawing, in the belief that all violence, contentious issues and strong emotions were to be avoided. He thought he was unaffected by it all, never sharing with anyone his thoughts and feelings on family life. Until now, that is. "I did well at school academically and I was always the quiet one good at sports and athletics. That was a saving grace I feel."

"Yes, I think it probably was." I was thinking how helpful physical exercise and exertion can be in dealing with depression, frustration and repressed violence in a non-harmful way. If Mac had not followed this path, he would be acting in the same way as his dad.

Mac went on to tell me he found relationships difficult and felt wary around everyone. "It is like I don't know or understand the rules of the game." As he said this he looked tremendously troubled and was gripping his hand into a fist. He continued to move around restlessly.

Inside, I sensed the complete isolation that Mac must experience every moment of his life. He must feel permanently on edge, wrong footed, out of step.

Mac continued, "Father and mother are now divorced and all contact with the past is gone, thank Christ. Mother is now outgoing. She's always been a good listener and genuine with her emotions and sharing them. I've noticed the little differences each time I go home. She's been in a stable relationship for 10 years and I marvel at the way she and her partner argue and disagree with one another while still maintaining a healthy, balanced relationship."

Then, as an afterthought, Mac said with a smile, "Can you still have boyfriends at 60? They have houses on each side of Glasgow, both with no intentions of moving. I feel very wary around her partner; the unconscious memory of my father afflicts me. According to my mum I am distant and very difficult to reach—I can relate to that."

"Ever since I've moved down south, mum has always maintained regular contact. She is constant, she supports me in whatever I decide to do, even when I deliberately ignore her and am angry towards her. She does not cry and she will answer my questions regarding her relationship with my father. She flies down from Scotland to visit me three or four times a year. I'm glad she invites herself because I don't know if I could ask her to visit as I'm not that confident about asking her for things I want."

"What is difficult about asking?"

Mac had a pained expression on his face now as if he could not talk. His mouth was open, trying to get the words out, and he started to stammer. This articulate man suddenly became like a hesitant child. And once again this important new development showed itself just as we were reaching the end of the session.

I suggested that we talk more about this next time. He glanced at me, a look of relief gradually coming into his eyes. He took a deep sigh, leaned forward and reached for his shoes.

"OK," he said quietly, lost in a world of his own.

A CHILD'S NEEDS NEGLECTED

As Mac sat there today, eyeing me with cold hateful eyes, my mind wandered back to the previous session where he had talked about his mum.

"Mac, you were talking about your mum in the last session and I would like you to tell me more about her, about your relationship with her."

Mac turned red. He looked restless and agitated and was muttering under his breath, "Fuck me... fuck me Bernie; this is difficult."

"What's difficult?"

Pain and frustration clouded his face as he tried desperately to communicate. He suddenly blurted out, "We didn't have a fucking relationship, that was just it."

After a long silence I asked, "What was 'just it' Mac? What do you mean?"

Mac's face started to twitch involuntarily. I felt that whatever he was going through must be huge. Finally he said, "The problem was she could never, ever, be there for me. But..." he started to breathe more heavily, move about more restlessly "... what made it worse, what made it so fucking worse, was at moments when I really needed her to comfort me, to reassure me, she wasn't there. She wanted *me* to comfort *her*." He spoke in a high pitched, exasperated voice.

"That must have been terrible, Mac. How did it make you feel?"

He thought for a moment and then started to stutter pitifully. "Like I was falling... round and round... into an abyss. Like in one of those dreams." As I looked at this huge man I saw him diminish into a terrorised little boy. It was very sad to see this level of suffering.

Mac looked totally drained so I suggested we rest for a while.

I had been somewhat surprised at the power and onslaught of the experience he related and could see no point in re-traumatising him further at that moment. Gradually Mac's colour started to normalise as he began to talk more easily again and there was a sense of relief about him. I just carried on the rest of the session with comforting small talk to help him to prepare for the outside world and the drive home.

As he left and as I started to reflect on the experiences he had shared with me I realised that this was only one aspect

of Mac's suffering. I wondered how he'd come through it so articulate and intact in many ways. He must be very strong because he had also been forced to deal with his father's hair-trigger violence. What must it have been like to grow up with all of that? At those moments of the dad's violence or Mac's need, his mother's emotional level was that of a traumatised little girl, so she went with her needs to Mac, blind to his need for comfort and reassurance. It made me wonder whether there had been violence and abuse in his mother's own upbringing.

I then started to list what I thought were the beliefs that governed Mac's life. They were:

1. No one's there for me
2. Trust no one
3. Depend only on yourself
4. Always be on guard

5. Never, ever, drop your guard and be vulnerable—that's when you get hurt.

He later admitted that he felt like he was in no man's land in the First World War, crawling between enemy lines with no protection and no defence between the trenches—facing certain death at any moment.

ON THE MARCH

On this particular evening Mac sat shoulders slumped, very heavily depressed and not talking at all. This, in turn, made me feel restless. After some time I decided to share my feelings of restlessness. Mac just looked at me contemptuously as if to say 'that's your problem'.

"I wonder if you feel like that inside, Mac?"

"Nope, I don't," he said, still fixing me with a stare.

About 10 minutes from the end of the session I made a clinical decision. "Mac, I am still feeling restless. Can you notice the heaviness in the room?"

Before I could finish he said disdainfully, "Yes, I noticed you're jumping about all over the place." There was a look of sadistic pleasure at my discomfort and a thin smile played across his face. The atmosphere in the room was becoming increasingly oppressive—so much so that it was somehow difficult to breathe. Mac was sitting still and very sullen. The unbearable heaviness was Mac's, I knew, and I decided I had contained it long enough.

So I got up and marched up and down the room saying, "Well, someone has to unblock it."

Mac was absolutely astonished. His eyes were wide open, body energy now alive, no more slumping. A smile came to his face. I carried on dutifully marching up and down the room in at a pace that was needed to release the restlessness and heaviness I was feeling.

"This is not in the manual!" Mac roared, tears of laughter streaming down his face as I continued marching up and down. Then he collapsed laughing.

I sat down. "That's done it I think." Now in front of me I had a new Mac, full of fun and warmth-connected.

All heaviness gone, he was energised and relaxed. He got up, still laughing, a look of wonderment and amazement on his face and as he said goodbye he waved in the friendliest manner he had ever shown towards me.

LIBERATION AND SPIRITUAL AWAKENING

During a following session Mac began telling me about a particular time at home.

"One evening, Bernie, the atmosphere was tense. My dad found a reason to pick on my mum. He shouted abuse at her, building himself up into a fury, then raised his hands to punch and slap her.

"I'd watched this scene in paralysed terror many times, but this time I felt different, I felt the terror. There was now something deeper, stronger in me fuelled by protective hatred and revenge. I faced my dad and said, 'NO MORE!' He looked astonished but I could feel every cell of my being vibrating with hatred and rage towards him. I was fifteen years old and wanted this to end now. My father stopped, looked at me for a moment and walked away. My mum looked too—nothing like this had ever happened before."

"Mac, you transcended any feelings of terror. You stood directly in front of your mum and gave your dad a look that said, 'NO, it ends here, now, today, your reign of terror is over'."

"Yes, that's it. Then I just stood there, calm, solid and centred."

The balance of power in the house had changed forever. Mac's courageous act was a spiritual awakening for him for he had connected with a power greater than his fears. He broke out into beads of sweat as he contemplated the dangerous thing he had done.

I was transfixed. It was a very dramatic session and the temperature in the room had shot up. I sat there humbled by Mac's trauma—by the exceptional way he had transcended his suffering to find a depth of spirituality in the face of terror.

We were now at the end of the session. Mac looked quite shaky as he was leaving. "Bye Mac," I said. "Bye," he replied, apparently miles away as he walked off.

When he had gone I reflected on a passage from Joseph Campbell's *Myths To Live By*, in which he quotes the German philosopher Arthur Schopenhauer:

"How is it, he [Schopenhauer] asks, that an individual can so forget himself and his own safety that he will put himself and his life in jeopardy to save another from death or pain—as though that other's life were his own, that other's danger his own? Such a one is then acting, Schopenhauer answers, out of an instinctive recognition of the truth that he and that other in fact are one. He had been moved not from the

lesser, secondary knowledge of himself as separate from others, but from an immediate experience of the greater, truer truth, that we are all one in the ground of our being. Schopenhauer's name for this motivation is "compassion," mitleid, and he identifies it as the one and only inspiration of inherently moral action. It is founded, in his view, in a metaphysically valid insight. For a moment one is selfless, boundless, without ego. And I have lately had occasion to think frequently of this word of Schopenhauer as I have watched on television newscasts those heroic helicopter rescues, under fire in Vietnam, of young men wounded in enemy territory: their fellows, forgetful of their own safety, putting their young lives in peril as though the lives to be rescued were their own. There, I would say—if we are looking truly for an example in our day—is an authentic rendition of the labour of love." [1]

This, I think, was precisely Mac's experience.

WATERSHIP DOWN AND BIGWIG'S SACRIFICE

At the tail-end of a recent session I had asked Mac if any film had moved him by touching on his experiences. He had replied matter-of-factly, though he had never mentioned it before, "Oh yes, *Watership Down*." So, I decided that I would continue this dialogue with him about the film.

When Mac arrived, he looked around the room, eyed me suspiciously and took in every detail. I was thinking he would have made a wonderful SAS soldier.

"Well," he said, and sighed.

---

1   *Uber die Grundlage der Moral*, essay by German philosopher Arthur Schopenhauer, 1839

He sat quietly, right hand seeming to jump and twitch until it turned into a customary fist.

"Mac, if you haven't got anything immediate, could we talk about your experience of watching *Watership Down?*"

He looked quite pleased. "Oh, yeah." He took a deep breath, sat back to get comfortable and released his fist. "Well, Bernie, it all feels so simple, so straightforward. A depiction of events in an animated cartoon involving rabbits struggling against injustice." Mac's face clouded over and the mood of the room changed.

"My memories, my unrecognised feelings, were brought into conscious awareness from watching *Watership Down.*" I felt fascinated that this big man who'd known almost the limits of human suffering had found help in a cartoon. For me this was a first. Mac went on, "I read the book when I was in my teens and even then it moved me greatly. It brought up such profound feelings about the battle for justice and freedom in the face of tyranny and terror."

Mac explained that the book *Watership Down* by Richard Adams, upon which the film is based, concerns a group of rabbits leaving their hitherto cosy but ultimately doomed warren and setting out in search of a new warren where they could live safely. He continued, "It's a story of self discovery, a venture of loyalty, trust, and for me the willingness to make a sacrifice in defence of individual rights."

Mac paused for a while: his face went a bit pale. He stared at the floor and continued, "What can I say, what can I do other than tell you my feelings surrounding the scene in which the two rabbits, Bigwig and General Wound-Wort fight for control? It may seem simple but the underlying theme is of great importance for me."

Mac swallowed. "Bigwig is one of those who leaves the established warren in search of a new place to live. Even though he is stronger, possesses knowledge of the world at large and has leadership experience, it's not him who leads the band but another rabbit called Hazel. Hazel possesses a quality that Bigwig is yet to realise. It's one of care and compassion for those around him no matter who they are. Bigwig reluctantly agrees to follow Hazel, but plans to usurp his leadership at the first opportunity."

I was truly fascinated at the unfolding of this story and Mac's complete comprehension of it. Mac continued, "The rabbits come face to face with an oppressive force in the shape of General Wound-Wort, intent on subjugating them and eradicating all independent rights." I noticed both Mac's hands had turned into fists, knuckles white. He was now breathing much faster. "General Wound-Wort runs his warren in military precision, maintained through a regime of harshness and terror." Mac's hate looked palpable now. "His word is law, above questioning and discussion. In short, he is a dictator."

I looked at the clock. Good, we still had quite a lot of time. Mac went on, "By the time of the confrontation, Bigwig has put to one side his leadership aspirations and is united with the other group members in defending themselves against the General and his vastly superior army of followers. The General is fierce, intent on destroying all those who oppose him. It is this scene which moves me greatly."

Mac paused, and I was on tenterhooks.

Mac said very firmly, "Bigwig faces up to the General, defending and protecting the group less able than he is. Although he is the biggest in the group, Bigwig is still smaller and no match for the General. Both rabbits know this, yet Bigwig stands by his decision to defend the group. In a crucial moment Bigwig acknowledges this and his loyalty to the group leader Hazel. For me it's symbolic of the battle for the right to be heard and to openly possess individual thoughts without intimidation or retribution. It is also about standing up for what is morally right."

I was transfixed by Mac's identification with the terror and oppressive ways of the General. Clearly this paralleled his feelings about his violent father.

Mac's voice broke. "The scene moves on and the tears are flowing down my cheeks. I recognise the significance of what I am watching and find it climactic and disturbing." Mac's face now looked flushed. "Bigwig's struggle, my struggle, all intertwined. A battle is raging in my heart, yet I understand Bigwig's motivation. It's in defence of others physically less able than himself and lies above and beyond any idea of personal gain or safety."

My mind immediately flashed back to Mac's confrontation with his father.

Mac's voice cracked now. "Such a sacrifice," he said, "such grief, such suffering. No person can ask that of another—it can only be undertaken voluntarily. Righteousness shall prevail but it takes courage to make it happen."

The hairs stood up on my arms. I was intensely moved at the emotional identification Mac had made with Bigwig facing the General, and himself at the age of 15 facing his dad to protect his mother. The clarity of that experience of sacrifice was being lived out in front of me. Mac went on, "In the blink of an eye, the understanding of what I had seen crystallised my memories and feelings. I felt deeply moved as I gained a new perspective on a major event in my life, a perspective that recognises and assigns."

Mac paused, looking out the window. I realised time was moving on. He continued, "The scene drew importance to my actions in a time of great terror. Understanding comes in many forms... it takes a willingness and desire to look deep within oneself to realise this. In the story Bigwig survives the battle with the General."

I looked up at the clock and noticed we were right on time. Mac looked emotionally drained. I felt how important this film had been to Mac's healing and liberation from his terrible suffering. As we got to the door Mac stopped, looked at me for the first time and said in a small voice, "Can I have a hug?"

"Sure," I said, and I noticed as I hugged him that his body was riddled with tension.

"Bye, Bernie, see you next week."

I closed the door feeling stunned at the enormity of what I had just heard.

MAC FACES DEATH

It was a dark, blustery evening when Mac arrived. He looked apprehensive as he walked in, his large frame and tall straight walk filling my hallway.

His eyes checked every aspect of the room. He was in deep thought as he did his customary ritual—shoes to the left with car keys inside them.

After Mac had agreed for his case study to go into this book, I used to write up his story at regular intervals and give it to him for his observations on accuracy and for his agreement. As a spin off, this gave the therapy greater depth.

Mac started by saying, "What you wrote about me and our session a few weeks ago helped me so much. It enabled me to cry, which I find extremely difficult."

"Do you have a support group?" I asked.

"Yes, that's where I took it. I read it out to a few of them." A wave of compassion went through me. He was referring to the case study for this book that I had given him for his approval. In it I had written about his supreme act of courage and sacrifice in facing up to his father to protect his mother.

"Bernie," Mac cried despairingly, "what's happening to me, I feel so confused?" He paused. "I am in chaos." He now had his head in his hands.

"I am here Mac. It's the shock coming out after all these years." Gently I asked, "Do you have any association that comes up around this chaos, any memory?"

Mac looked ashen. "I faced death and my mum and dad…" he paused, sighed, looking from side to side in utter exasperation…"they carried on around me…like I was not there. Fuck. What does she want from me?"

He got up now, pacing up and down and stuttering pitifully.

The energy that filled the room was titanic, oppressive. I breathed, relaxed, stayed in the moment to get a sense of peace in myself. To witness such suffering was an incredibly humbling experience.

Mac's colour started to return to his face. He looked calmer now.

"How do you feel?"

"I feel," Mac answered quietly "like the level of threat I was just experiencing has dropped."

"Much?"

"From about 100 per cent to 50 per cent."

"Yes, OK." Inside I still felt his radar scanning energy for danger, still active.

We both suddenly started coughing. The room was now sweltering and I was desperate to go to the toilet. I shared this with Mac who laughed in disbelief and relief at my disclosure. Ending time was near so I opened the patio doors to let in the crisp night air.

MAC'S LIFE AS OPERA

Mac arrived for his session looking as dark as thunder, glowering around the room. He looked at me with a sneer and then said, "I want to pick on something. I want to pick on you. Everything is wrong."

He went on in his strong Scottish accent, "I just can't get rid of it. I just can't get rid of it." He was moving his hands, flicking them, as though something was stuck to them. As he flicked his hands, he bared his teeth. He unconsciously brought up his right hand in a claw and growled.

I had the distinct feeling of 'unbearableness'. This

unbearable feeling was my sense of what was stuck to Mac. He can't get away from it whatever he does.

Mac looked at me contemptuously then looked away. He had started to remember things that had helped him from previous sessions. If he got up and paced, this would allow him to use up more of his energy. He said, "I am fucking getting up, I can't stand sitting here." He started to pace up and down, to claw and growl. I asked him to exaggerate the clawing and the growling because it seemed the best expression of the animalistic rage he felt. So, by expressing this, it could afford him at least some relief.

He said, "I am just so full of energy." I asked where this energy was.

"In my legs."

I had an idea, but as soon as I had it I also knew that Mac would not agree to it.

"Mac, there is something you can try if you like to, that might help."

"Yeah," he said sullenly, "what is it?"

"Well, if you lie on the floor and just let your legs express that energy in a running motion…"

Mac cut me off as I was speaking and regarded me with incredulity. As he looked at me with this questioning expression I felt a smile creeping up inside me.

"That's fucking mad. Do you think I'm going to lie down and fucking do that? How's that going to help me, pretending to fucking run?" Inside me the smile was growing bigger.

"Well, it's difficult to tell you the experience before you have it and to have it you have to do it."

I had found this technique helpful when working with women who had been raped. The trapped feeling in the legs is adrenaline, the fight or flight response. In the sense of running or by closing your eyes, you start to release that energy. This can often afford you some emotional relief and may trigger memories that are helpful.

"But you don't have to do it, it's your choice."

Mac sat down on the floor grudgingly. In a little boy's voice, he whined and rocked back and forth as he sat. "I'm not going to fucking do it. No, I'm not fucking doing it."

All of it was said like a child sulking and having a tantrum. Suddenly, he got up, and started marching up and down. Then he leant on the back of an arm chair, face now blood red, twisting his body into all sorts of awkward shapes and contortions. It was clear that there was some huge struggle going on inside him. Mac doesn't always tell me what he's struggling with inside, but he lets me facilitate him dealing with it.

"Boy," he said suddenly, "it's so hot in here. I'm sweating, my hands are sweating." Mac's colour can change dramatically within a given session and he now had a grey-like pallor that made him look quite unwell.

Having seen that struggle for so long I said, "Mac, it's been our experience in other sessions that physical contact helps you."

Mac looked at me and said, "I'm not coming over there." I moved forward about an inch to adjust my back. Mac, who was right across the room, glared at me with the clear message that I should stay where I was.

"I wondered what you were going to do then."

"Yes, I did slightly move, but I was adjusting my posture because I currently have a bad back."

Mac listened like he couldn't care less about my back. He stood there for a while, swaying backwards and forwards. Then he said, "I want to come over there but I can't. My legs won't move. I am rooted to the spot."

"OK, just stay there and if you don't come it doesn't matter."

Suddenly, Mac just walked over slowly and sat down like a little boy on the side of my armchair. I placed my hand gently on his left shoulder and asked, "Is that OK?" (It is so important to check with physical touch and not assume you are doing the right thing. The client will tell you.)

Mac whispered that it was, then a frightening thing happened. His whole face started to twitch involuntarily. He started to blink incredibly fast. I was greatly moved at seeing his suffering. I was so aware of all this turmoil in Mac's mind that I decided simply to stroke his hair in a gentle way, as you would a child. But I asked Mac first if that would be OK. He said 'yes' quietly. I hardly touched his hair but just enough to feel the contact of the stroke. Time was getting on now but Mac started to calm down, his twitching stopped slowly.

Mac decided to get up and sit in his usual chair opposite me. When he looked at me almost pleadingly and reached out as he had done before, I gently took his hand and looked into his eyes. He looked back to mine, searching. He had to see my care and it was important that he saw the sincerity in my eyes.

He saw the truth of what I felt for him and his suffering and seemed a little calmer, though still full of angst and despair. I had a momentary thought that the time was getting on now

139

and that we had to end. Because the room was sweltering on this summer evening, I imagined going out into my garden with Mac, letting him feel the cool night air, as I knew he liked the fountain with the Buddha presiding over it.

Mac noticed immediately and asked, "What happened there—how are you feeling? You looked uncomfortable. Are you bored?"

"No, Mac," I responded clearly and firmly, "I'm not bored. I was realising that we were about to run over time and we had to end the session, but at the same time I had the vision of the two of us walking out to the garden, to the fountain, to the Buddha I have in my garden."

What followed next was quite incredible. Mac smiled slowly with a look of total disbelief and pleasure mixed. He said, "That's fucking great." He then started to laugh, doubled up with real belly laughs. "Thank you. It's not what you said: it's that you told me what you were thinking."

With that I said, "Ok, let's be naughty," and we walked out together into the cool evening breeze, which was in such a marked contrast to the sweltering room. We were there only a few minutes until Mac turned to leave and we walked back together. He was laughing all the way, different energy, a different person altogether now.

As he got to the door, ready to go, this huge man of 6'2" looked down at my 5'2" and asked, "Can we have a hug?"

We hugged and I felt Mac's body tremble as though he had relaxed just that little bit more.

"Bye, Bernie," he said lightly, "see you next week," and carried on laughing as if he could not believe it.

WORMTONGUE AND GANDALF

It was about 6.50pm. Waiting for Mac to arrive, I recalled how in the previous session we had worked very much with his fear of silence, his whole approach to silence, how anxious it made him. We looked at it step by step and though Mac had found this very difficult and had tried to resist, in the end he said he felt as clean as a piece of pine. When I asked him whether that was good, bad or neutral, he said, "Oh, good." This is placid Mac. To get information from him about something like this is like pulling teeth. Nonetheless he clearly felt something important had happened in the session.

Unusually, in the last few weeks, Mac has sent me a couple of letters and a couple of emails. I was excited because he told me he had found *The Lord of the Rings* becoming more and more helpful to him. Previously Mac had only ever talked about *Watership Down*, so this introduction of a new film was very interesting.

When Mac arrived I noticed him move his face back just a couple of inches in his instinctive wariness. He carried out his ritual of looking round every inch of the room, checking everything, taking his shoes off and putting his car keys and wallet in his left shoe. He then gave me a look, somewhat searching and somewhat aggressive.

"What are those?" he asked, pointing to some throat pastels that I had on my right hand side, "dog biscuits or something?" The tone had a subtle edge of sarcasm and the lips very subtly curled as he spoke. If there is such a thing a semi snarl, this was it!

I just replied, "They're for my throat because it sometimes gets a bit irritated."

Mac said, "Oh," in a tone so markedly agreeable that there was quite a contrast with the tone of his opening words.

"Bernie, after our last session, something occurred to me—a way of seeing things." Mac was referring to imagery from *The Lord of the Rings* which he had mentioned to me briefly in previous sessions. "Wormtongue is the advisor to the King of Rohan, but his influence is much more powerful than that of advisor. He has the king under his control. As a result the king is wizened, feeble, weak and his eyesight is clouded over by cataracts. He speaks Wormtongue's words, and is unable to function independently. Wormtongue is an unhealthy influence, a poisoner and corrupter of minds."

I recalled that Grima Wormtongue's words constantly whispered in the king's ear had the effect of draining the king of any energy and autonomy. He became Wormtongue's puppet and remained in a kind of depressed stupor most of the time.

I thought how very interesting it was that this man in front of me, who could be reduced to pitiful stuttering, was so articulate and logical in communicating the intricacies and mood of this film.

Then Mac spoke of Gandalf the White, the Wizard for Good, who had the power to dispel Wormtongue's effect on the king.

"Gandalf releases the king's mind from the grip of Wormtongue's words, whereupon the king wakes up from his hypnotised state of mind, his eyesight clears and he regains control of himself and his physical strength. Now, free from the distorting influence of Wormtongue, the king wishes to hear Gandalf's opinion much to the bitter resentment of his advisor. Wormtongue, seen for the sly manipulator he is, finds himself cast out."

My question to Mac was, "Who is Wormtongue, who is Gandalf?"

He stood up. "I'm feeling restless."

"Good, just feel your energy and follow through." This was the pattern we used when Mac was becoming angry or restless. He looked across the room and made direct eye contact.

"Are you Gandalf?" he asked in a searching, testing way, as if I had suggested that I was.

I noticed a look on Mac's face of one who has set a trap for you and is pretty sure you are going to walk into it.

"What do you think?" I asked, paused for a moment and then slowly added, "That's what your mind has come up with."

He smiled slowly. "Touché." This answer indicated to me that I had not walked into his trap.

If I had agreed that I was Gandalf, I felt that Wormtongue and Gandalf would not have remained together as the negative and positive parts of Mac's psyche. He would not then have sensed his own power to put things right by tackling his inner Wormtongue.

Later, on the phone, referring to this session, Mac said he had found it "very deep—maybe too deep'. He wondered whether he should stop coming to see me.

"We can talk about that in the next session." I told him, as I had done at regular intervals, that I was concerned he was doing too much therapy. Independent of me, he was going to workshops and also seeing a craniosacral therapist. The personal impact on him of *The Lord of the Rings* as well as all this therapy made me fear he was overwhelming himself by bringing up too much powerful material.

I felt he should reduce his workshops so that when he left therapy he would know that he could function properly. I also talked about cutting down on the craniosacral therapy which, though quite gentle, can bring up a great deal. I suggested that he go to see his GP to get some prescriptive medicine to help him with the high level of anxiety he was feeling.

I also advised that he didn't have to be so stoic in facing all this horrible emotion. Quick as a flash Mac came back at me.

"Stoic. I'll have to look that up in my dictionary, Bernie," he said, annoyed.

"OK," I replied, "it means someone who is hard on themselves, who endures rather than seeks help. Be more compassionate to yourself. There is no reason why you can't go to the doctor and get some medication to temporarily help you through this period as you did before. You don't have to do it all on your own and you do need to be around more people who are not in therapy."

Now Mac seemed to want to get off the phone. "Bye," I said, "see you next week."

At our next session Mac told me something had happened to him a while after our phone call.

"It suddenly all passed, I felt totally better."

"You came out of your depression and the horrible feelings?" I asked.

"Yes," he said. "Not long after that the realisation of *The Lord of the Rings* and Gandalf came to me."

"So, it sounds like you've found your inner Gandalf who has answered the trance of your inner Wormtongue. Is that what's happened do you think?"

Mac looked at me, turned his head sideward, eyed me suspiciously and said, "You are being very slippery, Bernie."

"How?"

"Well, the things you are saying to me."

"Yes, I'm just saying things to you to see if they click or not. Only you know your inner truth and I am trying to help you to find it."

I was noting Mac's incredible awareness and his fear that I was trying to manipulate him—except that those words didn't form quickly enough for me to say that to him in the session.

Mac came and sat down, fixing me again with a stare.

"One of the scenes that keeps coming back to me, in *The Lord of the Rings*, is the mailed fist of the warrior who throws the ring into the air and catches it as he considers throwing it into the volcano." I noticed Mac doing the fist and catching the ring with his right hand unconsciously.

"Mac," I said, "can you keep doing that with your fist, opening and closing as you catch the ring, but really become it, really exaggerate it?" Mac did. "Stay with the feeling it gives you."

Mac looked very powerful now and said, "Fuck it, that's what it makes me feel. I know what I believe." A look of wonder passed across his face as I asked him to say that again. He did. "Fuck it!" he said more strongly, shoulders straightening up, jaw jutting out. He went very quiet and the look of wonder stayed on his face.

After a while he said, kind of to himself, "That's it...I realised sitting here that just before I felt better I let go of my depression. That was when I kept seeing that image."

"And those words?" I asked.

"Fuck it, I know what I believe."

"Is it your strength? Is that what helped you?"

"Yes," he said, "in retrospect it did."

"Mac," I inquired, "was it after this experience of your depression going that you had the insight about Wormtongue and Gandalf; and, if so, how long after?"

Mac's eyes were now wide like a little boy's. "Not long after, and I just had to email you and share it with you."

"But I am left still wondering if you found your inner Gandalf that gave you the strength to step out of your depression or your Wormtongue trance. Just something for you to think on or reject, Mac."

Mac eyed me suspiciously, and then looked softly at me, showing a great deal of affection. He then said, "Bernie, you are the X factor in this, in my healing."

"Oh," I said, "do you know how I am?"

"Not yet," he said.

"Oh well, there is no rush."

Mac's face flitted to anger and kindness in a split second as he said to me, "I didn't know whether to give you a slap or kiss you when you said that." Inside I was a little surprised, but felt very comfortable.

"Do you feel like that in a lot of your relationships? That is, you often feel you don't know whether to slap or kiss anyone?" Mac's face clouded over. He sighed, and with a sense of relief said, "All the time Bernie, all the time." There was such weariness now and sadness in his tone. I felt very moved for him.

"All I feel is dissatisfaction. How long? How long?" he cried out. "I've been doing all this stuff for five years—maybe longer. Two and a half years with Steve, my previous therapist, four years of weekend primary integration workshops, nearly two years with you, and I still feel dissatisfied."

"Mac, can you tell me what you feel behind that statement you've just made? What are the feelings? What are the words, if you can find any?"

He looked at me with resignation." It's inevitable."

"Is there more to that?"

"Yes," he said, "it will always be there. It's inevitable."

"There," I said quite firmly, "is the negative belief that brings all that feeling about. That is Wormtongue in you speaking. If you believe it won't change, it won't. If you believe it will change, it will. We have to focus on that negative belief that causes you so much suffering."

Inside I was experiencing some very uncomfortable feelings I couldn't define. Then Mac said, "You are the X factor in this. You always give me something, always meet me at whatever depth I am in myself. You are not fazed with anything I throw at you."

As if on cue, I looked at the clock and saw that we are just about to go over time. Mac knew this too but would push me a little longer if I let him.

"Oh well, thank you Mac," I said. "We are coming to the end now."

He got ready slowly and said goodbye. I was left with a kind of sick numbness in my chest. I shuddered, thinking, So this is what it feels like to be Mac.

MAC CONFRONTS HIS SUB-PERSONALITIES

Mac arrived today looking restless and angry. Before he sat down he couldn't wait to say to me, "I want to find something wrong—to find things wrong here. I want to argue with you."

As he sat down, he hit the Buddha that I'd lent him on the head with his hand, many times over, seemingly unaware of doing it. He had told me in previous sessions that he takes the Buddha to his weekend workshops on primal integration and calls it Bernie. It represents me.

I think I am going to tell him what I am seeing him do. I said, "Mac, do you realise that you are hitting the Buddha that you tell me represents me? How angry you are with me—but you don't show it here. You split off at these weekend workshops and once again I am encouraging you not to do that but to show me now." Mac stared back at me in vibrant, sneering contempt. Inside I was thinking, 'yes, he's angry with me alright'.

Realising this huge man had all this anger running through him, I suggested that he get up and pace, using up this energy.

"Why?" he sneered back at me. "Are you bothered or something? What's behind your suggestion?" He was staring hatefully at me.

"You seem to be overwhelmed with this anger and pacing has helped you in past sessions." Mac looked at me and started pacing up and down.

Then he said, "I want to kill, I want to destroy, I want to crush. I don't want any fucking sensitivity. Pooffy or nice, I want mechanical things that are heavy or strong. I want thick strong buildings that withstand anything."

He reminds me of the Nazis and worshipping the will. The room was stifling as he marched up and down, clawing at the air and growling and spitting out venomous, poisonous profanities. He was caught up in animalistic revulsion—the beast in him as he called it.

He looked up and said, "I feel like I'm possessed." My reaction was to see this hate as a burning acid fuelling the primeval savagery.

Then suddenly, after expressing all of this, hands shaking, face white, he looked at me like a frightened little boy with a kind of pleading in his eyes. He lowered his head a bit and asked, "Can I sit down next to you?"

Mac sat down like a child to the left side of my armchair. He wanted my hand on his shoulder, contact for reassurance to ground him. After a while he said, "I feel like I need some body work. If I lie down this energy will be OK."

"Alright," I said, and he lay down, face flinching. After a while he added, "I feel it will help if you put your finger in the middle of my forehead."

"Third eye?" I asked.

He just smiled. I gently circled his mid-forehead with my finger. For a while his whole body shook and twitched, then he calmed down and his breathing normalised.

Looking calmer, he decided to sit up.

"I split them off."

"Who?"

"My own personal Jekyll and Hyde."

This was Mac's reference to one side of him being a small boy and one side being his dad. His sub-personalities. He looked very serene as he got up, took his keys out of his shoes, put his wallet in his pocket and left.

Following this session I received an email from Mac:

"Bernie,

"I had a mindful of images last night, all revolving around hunger and emotional need. The first one is right at the forefront of my conscious mind—it's the scene from The Lord of the Rings *when the story of the ring's near-destruction is being retold. Men and Elves have united to fight Sauron and his demon allies. They have managed to chop the ring from his hand in the midst of battle.*

"It falls upon the King of Men to hurl the ring into the volcano, the only thing which can destroy its power. But the King of Men falters and decides against all that has been agreed and decides to keep the ring for himself. The Elvin Lord is at his side on the brink of the volcano's mouth and urges the king to adhere to the original agreement. He witnesses this change and through his grimy, battle-strained, sweat-covered face, the disbelief, the disappointment, the sheer frustration becomes visible.

"This scene is etched on my mind, frozen in time. The look upon his face (it's the same Australian actor who plays the Agent in the film The Matrix) *is one I identify with. Battling so hard, risking life and limb, forming alliances, united in struggling against a common evil, only to be cruelly let down at the crucial moment. What trust can be formed following such a devastating betrayal?*

"The other thing, which is running through my mind in close parallel, is being gunned down in no man's land. In my most vulnerable

of states, reaching out for help only to have the person I am attempting to approach, turn on me, gun me down. In my mind, she shows no pity for my state. I hate her cruelty, her laughter at my distress. I feel betrayed, never dare trust so willingly again, be suspicious of her. Fucking bitch. Whore. Die in hell. I'll never let you hurt me again."

In the email Mac was firstly alluding to his negative experience with his mother in trying to help her from his father's violence and, secondly, to the time he stood up to his father.

Following this brave, courageous act of speaking out and protecting his mother, his parents acted normally around him and he was astounded that no one noticed. It took a supreme effort of will and courage for him to face the terror of his father. No-one noticed his need afterwards to be held and reassured. That was what he meant when he talked of being left in 'no man's land'.

His mum needed him desperately but she could never meet any of his needs. That was terrifying to the lonely Mac. Once again she was not there for him. She had not noticed him.

FEAR OF SILENCE

Mac came today looking very disturbed and uncomfortable. After a while, he said, "Fuck it, I find it so difficult to be in groups." He paused, thought, and then said, "And in one to one sessions really, when I think about it."

"Can you say what it is you find so difficult?"

He paused for a while and then said, "I cannot deal with the silences."

"What happens?"

"I feel a massive pressure to end the silence."

"Why is it so important to end the silence?"

"Because I panic. It's desperation to find something to talk about and, if I can't, it creates panic."

"Do you share with anybody how you feel? With close friends?"

"I have done this with a couple of them, but it doesn't help."

"It doesn't help at all?"

"Not at all."

Inside I could feel the sense of being stuck and panic and the sense of not knowing what to do arising in me. It was clearly the experience that Mac had.

Mac then continued quite loudly, "I feel trapped, lost, like there's no way out'."

"And then what happens?"

"I feel so stifled, so inhibited. I cannot wait to remove myself from that situation. I walk away."

"Mac," I said, grabbing a piece of paper and a pen, "let's observe and track your process around silence step by step and I'll write it down."

Mac gave me a look as if to say, 'how is that going to help?'

"OK. If we write down your process, you'll be able to witness it, observe it, and see how it happens, step by step, from a different perspective. That's its value and I'll give you the paper afterwards."

Mac nodded his head in agreement.

"First, Mac, you experience silence in a conversation. I

want you to really put yourself in a situation and tell me what happens next."

"...Pressure to end the silence."

"Anything else?"

"If I'm asked to do something, I ascribe a gravity to it that's completely out of proportion."

"How does that make you feel?"

"Crushed. My heart starts sinking. I'm going to be disappointed."

He paused for a while looking like a little boy, very scared, then continued, "I feel powerless." His voice now sounded very young. "Scared that I can't..." He stopped in mid-sentence, eyes starting to blink rapidly, face flinching and contorting.

"... Wanting the violence to end. Not being able to escape that situation."

"Carry on, Mac. "I know it's difficult."

"Acute physiology of fear and suspicion, refusing to comply with what's being asked of me."

"Anything more?"

"I'm paralysed inside, frightened to move."

"This is obviously bringing up all that happened in your childhood."

"Yes," he said in a whisper, as if we shouldn't be heard.

"Mac, can you remember what happened prior to one of your dad's violent outbursts?"

He cringed a bit as he took himself back there. Then a flash of insight passed across his face. "Yes," he said a little excited, "there was a strange quietness and I always knew he was going to explode by that strange quietness, before it happened."

"Mac, could we say silence, that strange silence?"

"Yes," he nodded as he took in the memory of that silence.

"Mac, I'm wondering, if you interpret all silences now like you did when you were a little boy, whether silence equals violence."

He started to go white and perspire slightly. "Fuck it! That's it!" Again he said, "That's it. Fuck it. I always knew when he was going to go."

"And now you interpret any kind of silence as the prelude to danger and violence."

He looked astonished in the realisation of the unconscious effects of his trauma and the legacy and difficulty it had left him with in relationships. He sat back, kind of relaxed. After giving him some space I asked him how he felt.

"Like a clean piece of Ikea pine."

"Is that good or bad?"

"Oh, good." He mumbled almost as if he didn't want to say it. Sometimes getting information out of Mac was like pulling teeth.

A QUESTION OF POWER

Mac sat there today with a snarl on his face. The bag that had been fitted because of my tumour grumbled and made various noises. Mac looked at me very sternly and pointed to that part of me. "What's it doing when it does that?" he asked in a very irritated fashion.

I said, "I will tell you, but I'm very interested to know what you will get from knowing?"

Mac just looked at me in a very surly manner. "I just want to know!"

"But what will it give you to know Mac?"

Mac clinched his right fist, leaned forward and said to me in the coldest way, "I want to see you squirm."

"OK, what will it give you to see me squirm?"

Mac exploded, "I want to break your fucking confidence. You're so fucking confident as you sit there."

"So you break my confidence, Mac, what does that give you?"

"I would be on top."

"So, it's a question of power in this relationship?"

"Yes," he said vehemently.

He went very quiet and after a while looked up and said, "Why do I do that sort of thing? How can I be so cruel?"

"Because that part of your dad and his cruelty you experienced is what you are now capable of doing to others."

"But I don't want to."

"But you do and that's what you just did. It's better to invite that part of yourself into the room and start to accept that you can be cruel. We will work with it in our relationship, rather than deny it and have it explode and be out of your control."

Mac looked at me and said, "I want to cry."

"This saying has just come to me, Mac, and I'm going to tell you what it is. When Jesus was on the cross and he was being cruelly persecuted and tortured he said, 'Forgive them, they know not what they do'. And now, Mac, you do know what you do. Unlike the people in Jesus' time, you now start to have a choice about whether you keep on doing it."

This was a most amazing experience with Mac's cruelty. When he left I'd never felt so good—so completely whole, safe and strong. I was surprised that there was no anger. In fact, it felt like I had somehow been given a gift in Mac's showing me my own strength to deal with my experience of cancer. Since that session, this feeling has never left me. So in a strange way I am grateful to Mac, which I am sure would astound him. However, I don't see myself telling him!

STAR WARS AND DARTH VADER

Mac came today. He didn't look his usual smart self. It was as if he wasn't looking after himself. He came in quietly and sat down for a while, carrying on from the end of our last session where he had become quite aggressive with me. He leaned forward, chin jutting out and snarled at me.

"You're not going to change me." He looked at me challengingly and confrontationally.

"Do you think I want to?"

He nodded to himself.

"No, you want to change. That is why you come here."

What I was working with was showing Mac how he bullies others and parts of himself. Mac sat there. I asked, "Could you go inside Mac?" as he has a good facility for imagery.

Mac quietly went inside. His face moved with pain.

"There's a wax figure melting," he said, breathing faster. "I'm trying to hold it, to pick up the pieces, stop them melting, but as they melt they are running on the floor, going down the drain."

Surprisingly Mac, who doesn't cry very often, started crying in deep despair. "As it was going down the drain I felt helpless that I couldn't stop it." He waited a while and looked quite frightened. "I feel as if I'm engulfed in black swirling darkness down this drain. Terror deeper and deeper. It's a terrifying abuse." Mac now cried out, "Will he come, will he come, the guardian angel?" He paused, crying, "Will he come? The knight on the white charger, will he rescue me?"

Then he collapsed into the chair with the slow realisation that nobody had come to rescue him. As he sat there in utter aloneness, despair and resignation, I had been holding my breath. As I let go of my breath, my chest wheezed. Mac, to my amazement, smiled and looked comforted. His eyes moved as if he were following something.

He stared into my eyes with a look that was soft and warm. "When you wheezed just now it reminded me of Sandy."

"Sandy?"

"Sandy, my dog. He always used to make that noise when he lay down and stretched out. I find that very comforting."

It's very mysterious how the unconscious works sometimes. Suddenly Mac's inner image changed to what he described as 'a house out on the flatlands like in America'. At the same time, he said, the song by the Pussy Cat Dolls called *Don't you wish your girlfriend was hot like me?* was going through his mind. As Mac looked at the house a wind was roaring through it.

I asked, "Is it vacuuming the dust of distress?"

Mac smiled, nodded. "Yes, a spring clean." He looked comfortable for a while before his face clouded over. "There's a room I've never been in. It's at the top of the house."

"Can you go in?" I gently guided.

"I'm frightened." After a pause, he went in and shuddered.

"It's like a psycho's house. A house of pain and cruelty. It's so dark." He paused again; his face had gone quite white. Then he said, "It's like Darth Vader."

"Can you just look at him, Mac?" I asked, feeling what he felt.

Suddenly Mac looked relieved. "It's all changed. It's exactly like the scene at the end of *Star Wars*, where Darth Vader is no longer himself. He is Anakin now, about 60 years old.

"I keep hearing these words, 'an absence of threat, an absence of threat'." Mac's face looked profoundly relieved and curious.

After a long pause, in a tone with an expression of someone who finds the answer to something troubling him deeply, he said, "That's it—that's what she represents. No threat. An absence of threat."

"Are you referring to your girlfriend Lara?"

"Yes." He smiled the gentlest smile I've seen from him.

This was a most important moment as it was his first ever experience of not being under threat. His whole early life had been lived in an atmosphere of terror, of real and impending violence with no escape. He had never known anything else until this wonderful magical moment that his girlfriend, the first he had ever lived with, so transformatively represented. While he reacted with titanic rage, irritation and claustrophobic tension to the inadequacies and behaviour of Lara that so disturbed him, he loved her. Now he knew why. She had given him the greatest gift of his life, an absence of threat.

"Mac," I said after I had allowed him the time to savour this marvellous moment, "what's happened?"

"The Pussy Cat Dolls are still singing."

"Does it connect with you at all?" I asked this because I knew the song *Don't you wish your girlfriend was hot like me?* had been haunting Mac and disturbing him until now. In fact he now knew he didn't wish his girlfriend to be a lot like the song. She'd given him the absence of threat.

As Mac sat there he said, "My image of the Darth Vader family portrait has come up again."

"Can you look at Darth Vader? Anakin as he is now. Can you look at Anakin?"

"Yes."

"Can you enter Anakin? Become him?"

Mac said that if he moved near him in his imagination, he was drawn to his eyes, but when he looked they were very powerful, like a black hole. He was frightened to enter and become Anakin.

"I know it's frightening but I'm here. See what happens if you can."

"The eyes are black: they are drawing me in." He went in and his voice became small like a little boy's. "Its like a huge black cave in here. Absolutely black."

"It's OK, Mac, I'm here."

Suddenly he looked relieved. "There are diamonds in the ceiling and everywhere—it's like a starry night."

Then he started to cry, really sob, tears running down his cheeks as he exclaimed, "This is too good for me, this is too good for me."

I think the experience of absence with no threat and the sense of no tension and the beautiful picture was too much for Mac. He had never known any of this in his life.

He said Sandy was back, happily sniffing around, curious as always.

I connected this to Mac as I talked to him. "So Sandy is just happy and curious. Are you still anxious?"

"Yes, it's all great but there is something else now. I just feel angry. I just feel angry." Once again he looked forlorn.

"Can you have an attitude of embracing the anger too, so it's not an outsider? It's embraced, not abandoned? Last week when we worked with your anger, we discussed how tired it was, how weary it was."

160

Mac did this and then calmed right down, very still and just said in a whisper, "Diamonds in the dark, diamonds in the dark."

As he settled down, I looked at the clock and saw we had about ten minutes to go. It seemed a much longer journey. Mac's very powerful imagination can be used for his healing but if there are frightening images, he gets extremely scared. As he started to come gently back into the room, into the here and now, he looked at me and said, "It was a very powerful session last week and, when I went, it seemed to affect Lara. I think she will go for therapy and that's helpful.

"As you start to change inside, it will affect the dynamics of your relationship."

He told me she had cried a lot when he had met her last week and told him things she'd never spoken of before about being bullied.

As it came to the end of the session, the room felt quiet and warm and Mac looked across to me, staring straight into my eyes with the softest smile. "Thank you, thank you Bernie."

As he slowly left, I came back into the room which was quiet and warm. It seemed that the softest smile could permeate the room.

"Amen, our Father," I started saying quite quietly. Something important just happened here.

READY TO LET GO

Unfortunately about this time I had to go in for my final operation. I was in hospital for about a month and expected to be unable to work for at least for four to six weeks. Previously, I had explained to Mac that I would be unavailable for a time and that if he needed to find another therapist I would understand. But after that period Mac came back and we had a good few sessions together. He seemed much better for the break and had been able to integrate a lot of the work we had done together.

Now on his own, he had gained more confidence in dealing with the emotional issues he had experienced. But there was one significant change. Mac's relationship seemed to be very healthy for him and he was receiving much support; so he decided to end therapy, with the proviso that he could always come back.

20 MOVIE THERAPY

Having shown some cases in which I have used movie therapy, I thought I should explain more specifically exactly what movie therapy is.

We have all seen movies and felt sad or happy after watching them. I have taken this process further, developing the theory that movies can actually help with a range of deep seated problems.

Along the way, when I was listening to a client talking, a scene from a film would suddenly flash across my mind. I didn't really use this at first, as I was not confident enough; but it really started me thinking, and that was how my work on movie therapy began. Nowadays, by encouraging people to examine their chosen films as part of their therapy, I have found I can help them unlock their traumas by finding the therapeutically needed moment in their film.

I have found that moments from movies, issues contained within them or relationships between movie characters, have helped many of my clients quickly to identify the feelings, and later the reasons, for unconscious unhappiness. So many times a scene has proved a powerful catalyst for releasing unconscious, repressed emotions and memories. Seeing a mirror image on screen has assisted clients enormously in realising and communicating troubling emotions. Using film as an aid to healing, they have gone on to lead much more contented and rewarding lives.

My focus is on the balanced growth of my clients' spiritual and psychological development. As part of the clients' therapy I teach them how to develop their awareness to establish mindfulness. Mindfulness is the ability to witness our thoughts, our feelings and our bodily sensations from a detached point of view so we get to observe how they work inside—their process.

What has been especially helpful in assisting clients to be mindful of their process is when I give them "homework". I ask them to watch a DVD of a film they have chosen containing scenes which particularly move them. The process I teach them enables them be mindful of their response and to view these scenes repeatedly, gradually reducing the emotional charge from them. Any further emotional expression that may be needed can be worked on in therapy and can include the discovery of further insights.

As I began gradually to work more and more with film I decided that the media would be a very important avenue to raise public consciousness of the power and potential of movies. I wanted people to appreciate that, while a film could be for their enjoyment at home, it could equally take them on a journey of self discovery, helping them to deal with issues that they were struggling with in their life and relationships. By bringing these issues to the surface for them, a film could also assist in any therapy or counselling they might be undergoing.

Interestingly, people can also experience the power of film without being conscious of it. They may not even connect material that disturbs them with a movie they have seen two or three days before.

I have also tried to use the media as a platform from which to address film-makers, film companies and advertisers. Their work has an enormous impact on the world that we live in, helping to shape morality and standards, and they carry the moral responsibility that goes with that. I have tried to make the case that there is no reason why films that heal, tell real stories and are a positive influence cannot be good box office too.

One of the dilemmas I have faced is that the media tend to trivialise or sensationalise what I am doing, either through misrepresentation or through wanting to entertain their viewers and listeners rather than interest and inform them. So I have had to walk a fine line between publicising movie therapy and making clear it is not a gimmick.

AGONY UNCLE

My experience with *Chat* magazine was a case in point. *Chat* published an interview with me and went on to give me a column. The idea was that readers were encouraged to write in with their problems and I would suggest films that might help them. But as I didn't know them my objective was to give them the idea of using films as a resource, like books, so that they could themselves find films to help them. They would know when they found the films that were right for them by the magic emotional moments of tears, anger or of happiness that their chosen films produced in them. They would know because they were the experts on their own lives.

I thought the column was worth a trial run, especially as *Chat* had a weekly circulation of a million and a readership of 2 million. However, I hit quite an important snag as reporters and editors were adapting to their own style the words coming out under my name. I felt I was being misrepresented so I withdrew from the column immediately. It was an amicable ending and they understood the reason for my decision.

What I learned from this experience and from subsequent interviews was that I had no control over what a reporter might write or what an editor might decide to edit. I concluded that I had to find ways of speaking directly to the public in my own words so that my message was not sensationalised or trivialised and so I could also make clear what movie therapy is and what it isn't.

A news team from the BBC came to interview me. She was a real 'Sloane Ranger' and I didn't like her manner, so I said to her: "We don't have to do this interview—in fact, we can call it a day now." I stressed that movie therapy was more than flavour of the month and that I didn't want her to diminish or trivialise what I was saying about my work. A few minutes later she came over to me and said she was sorry if she had offended me.

I said to her "Do you have a film?" and she answered very angrily and defensively, "Don't get me on films." When I asked her why, she went very quiet, then said, "There is a film." It turned out to be *The Railway Children*. I asked her what it was about the film, and this very sophisticated woman started to sob.

It emerged that what had moved her was the scene where the girl was waiting for her father and couldn't see him for the steam of the train that had pulled in. It was this moment of apprehension and fear that spoke to the memories of this reporter. Apparently when she was little, her father had been a military man, often away, and she had missed him tremendously. She'd been in that position of waiting and wondering whether he'd come home and seeing that film had brought back a great deal to her. She ended up giving one of the best and most honest television reports on my work I'd ever had.

Other journalists have had similar experiences and glimpses into what movie therapy can do. Some years ago a reporter from the *Daily Express* asked me to explain what movie therapy was and instead I suggested that a better way for him to write about it would be for him to experience it. His film was *Far from the Madding Crowd*. He said he had been really moved by the choice that Julie Christie's character, Bathsheba Everdine, had made in going for a soldier as opposed to a down-to-earth country lad.

When I asked whether he had perhaps been faced with a similar situation in his own life he nodded and looked down. I then asked him if he had any sensations at that moment in his body. He said his stomach felt uncomfortable and seemed very surprised. I decided to stop then as I did not want him to make a disclosure about his personal life that he might regret afterwards but he'd had a glimpse of the power of movies in a therapeutic situation. Recently another reporter from the *Daily Express* had a whole one-hour session with me, and her account is such an accurate record that I'm including it here:

Slouched in an armchair, my right hand is numb and my left foot keeps twitching. I'm talking about the 1985 film The Breakfast Club *to psychotherapist Bernie Wooder, who has pioneered movie therapy in the UK.*

"We have all watched films and felt sad or happy afterwards," *says Wooder in his book* Movie Therapy: How It Changes Lives. *He explains that an on-screen image can provide a way to discuss strong emotions and memories. As a cinema buff who regularly writes film reviews I liked the idea of looking at films in a new way but that wasn't the only attraction.*

I have always admired people who visit therapists because I couldn't imagine opening my heart to a stranger. However when I heard about movie therapy I realised that instead of talking about myself I could talk about films.

Wooder explains that movie therapy is not a quick fix. It may involve bringing difficult feelings to the surface and as a result can be upsetting. He asks if there's a film that speaks to me in particular. I tell him I identify with Allison in The Breakfast Club, *a film in which five teenagers from different cliques are stuck in detention together. Allison is the outsider.*

"I was bullied at school," I explain. "I felt like a nobody. I'm scared of that happening again."

He asks if I am feeling any physical sensations. I'm not and I worry that the question is a bit "new agey".

I recall a classroom incident. I was wearing a scarf and two boys grabbed the ends and pulled. I thought the teacher saw but he didn't do anything.

"If somebody did that now I would be angry," I say, "but I wasn't at the time. I just felt helpless."

Wooder asks again about any physical sensations I may be feeling. As I explain how I compensate for having been a shy, awkward child by being a forthright, bolshy adult, I realise my right hand is pulsing with energy. Now this I wasn't expecting. I ask if it is normal to have a physical reaction and he says it is.

Wooder explains it's because emotional feelings affect your body not just your brain.

"Your body manifests emotion denied by your mind. It feels emotion and lets you know," he says.

We talk about how The Breakfast Club *unfolds on a Saturday. On Monday everything will go back to normal and I realise I'm afraid that will happen to me. I'm content with my relationship, friends and career but I'm scared of losing it all. Wooder points out that my left foot keeps twitching as I talk.*

My ex-fiancé cheated on me after nearly seven years together. I was determined to get on with life and be happy but it hasn't always been easy. Wooder observes: "I have a sense you can't feel safe in your life. You think that Monday is going to come again." It's the perfect description of how I feel. I'm happier these days but I'm not at peace with events in the past.

"I feel my life is a notebook and there are pages I want to rip out," I say. Wooder asks if I have seen the 1998 film Sliding Doors *in which Gwyneth Paltrow stars as a woman whose life plays out differently in two parallel universes. I have seen it and tell him that I feel I want to "see behind the other door but can't".*

"Sometimes I go through a door without realising I have a choice until it's too late," I continue.

Wooder asks how my hand feels now and I realise it has gone numb. He asks me to think about The Breakfast Club *again and I explain that I'm annoyed with Allison. He suggests: "You can see her stuck in a cycle and know she will regret it one day. She doesn't do anything to change her life."*

I agree and add: "I feel I could have had a better time if I had tried." I explain that I wish I could wipe parts of my memory like in the film Eternal Sunshine Of The Spotless Mind, *in which Kate*

Winslet and Jim Carrey have their memories erased, though it hits me later that they both regret it.

I tell Wooder I'm not sure why I can't simply enjoy my life. He says I feel I have to be on guard which prevents me relaxing.

"Imagine you're walking along the street," he says. "You see a little girl. She's upset. You ask her what's wrong and she tells you she's frightened and lonely. What would you say to her?"

I have trouble answering but say I would walk along with her.

"I don't like imagining old me and young me. It's not that I want to leave her to be miserable," I say, "but I need to take her back home." Wooder thinks I don't know how to reassure her. In truth I want someone else to do it for me.

"Go back to a film," says Wooder.

A strong image comes into my head from a recently released movie I watched just a few days ago. In the movie Is Anybody There, Michael Caine is an elderly magician put in a care home. He befriends the young boy whose parents run it. Recalling their friendship I find it much easier to imagine old me and young me. We're on a beach getting an ice cream.

"The little girl would like that," says Wooder.

Walking out into the sunshine after our session I feel light and floaty as if I've had a massage or too much champagne. I never expected movie therapy to be such a physical experience. I walk past a newsagent and breaking into a smile I go in and buy an ice lolly.

Movie therapy helped me voice feelings I hadn't been able to describe before. It won't be right for everyone and you may need a few sessions. As with all kinds of therapy it can involve feeling worse before you feel better and can be very hard emotionally but I can say for certain that it helped.

One radio interviewer began crying on air as soon as we started talking about the film starring James Stewart *It's a Wonderful Life* in which an angel helps a despairing businessman by showing him what life would have been like if he never existed. I couldn't get to what had prompted this reaction as we were on air but the incident proved how quickly films can touch peoples' lives.

Despite the fact that when it first came out *It's a Wonderful Life* was a flop, the son of director Frank Capra said his father had received hundreds of letters from people who had been moved by it. In many cases it had changed their lives and had even stopped some people from committing suicide. A number of these letters were from inmates of San Quentin prison in the US who were living life at the sharp end.

When the Klu Klux Klan saw DW Griffith's film *Birth of a Nation,* they felt they had found the answer to their meagre 4,000 membership. They decided to use the film as a recruiting ad at all their rallies. A year later, their membership had risen to exceed 156,000. So uspet and embarrassed were the studios and DW Griffith himself that they made the film *Intolerance,* about the prejudiced attitude towards Irish immigrants, who at that time flooded to America and literally built much of it. The film was meant to counterbalance *Birth of Nation* and the way it had been presented by the Klu Klux Klan. It also must be borne in mind that at that time the heads of most Hollywood film studios were European Jews, who were obviously aghast at the racism being connected with their film.

I was being interviewed by BBC Isle of Wight. The interviewer was quite camp; he introduced me by saying, "Here we have Bernie Wooder, the movie therapist." Then he caught me on the hop. "Bernie, my favourite film—I must tell you straight away—is *Shaving Ryan's Privates*".

Once a listener called in after a radio programme to tell me how much she supported what I was doing, and talked about her own experiences. Problems with her legs had caused her great pain, anxiety and distress. She told me she'd been to see an old film directed by Charlie Chaplin, called *Limelight* about a ballet dancer played by Claire Bloom.

In one scene the dancer has an attack of nerves and says she simply cannot perform. Chaplin, playing the fading comedian and her mentor, gives her a stern look. The listener said this look had made her pull herself together, despite the fact that she had previously been contemplating suicide.

"It was as though he was talking directly to me," she told me, and continued, "Many years later I met Claire Bloom at a party, and I told her the story of Chaplin's effect on me. Claire said she wasn't surprised, because he'd had a similar effect when she acted with him in *Limelight.* She said no one before or since had had that effect on her.

On another radio phone-in a woman said she hated the film *The Piano.* Such a reaction is very interesting, as it is usually a result of a film evoking feelings that the person has been trying to suppress. She emailed me some months later and said she'd hated it because many of the emotions shown in the film paralleled the break up of her own marriage. Now she could view it and see with hindsight why she had found it so painful to watch.

No one size fits all when it comes to my work with movie therapy. Each individual needs to find their own film. Films are emotional nourishment, giving direction, showing another viewpoint, highlighting problems and presenting role models. They can help people communicate and identify feelings they can't name. Through the work I have done I hope gradually to raise people's consciousness of the power of films and teach them how to use films to heal themselves.

Of all the stories we hear or see, the most important are those we tell to ourselves. The problem for most people is that they remain unaware of these stories that they are telling themselves, and of the effect they have on their lives. These 'inner movies' are only glimpsed in powerful snapshots and flashbacks; but their effect on our emotions can be either devastating or liberating.

The problem of the inner movie is that it runs on insidiously, tenaciously, behind our back, so that we remain unaware of its corrosive role. A real movie—even a small moment from it—can at a crucial moment make a connection with the inner movie, and be the catalyst for bringing the unconcious into the concious. The repressed memory can be brought into the open, emotionally expressed, and resolved through awareness of its significance.

As I work together with my clients, their stories, their inner movies, gradually reveal themselves. People make decisions about themselves—for example, they persecute themselves over something about which they feel guilty. Their internal dialogue acts as an continuous inner critic which overwhelms them: it goes to create the emotional world in which they live: their own private suffering. All this contributes to creating and sustaining unconcious patterns of unhappiness, from which there seems no escape. Thus we create our own horror movies, of which we are the writers and directors. And much of what shapes our perceptions and emotional responses was our early childhood experiences. If those experiences were of abandonment, loss, cruelty, alcoholic- or drug-addicted parents, there will obviously be large areas of healing that need now to be met and nourished.

My aim is in this sense to become a co-director with my client, so that we can together in helping the client choose a healthier and more creative future.

21 MGM AND THE MEDIA ROLLERCOASTER

The phone rang one day and the caller introduced herself as a public relations executive for MGM and Warner Brothers.

"We've read about your work and are very impressed. We wondered if you would be interested in doing something for MGM on its 50th anniversary of *The Wizard of Oz*, which is being re-issued and digitally re-mastered?"

Would I! I thought. *"Bernie boy, you're on your way—wow!"*

"Yes," I said, "I could do a therapeutic perspective on *The Wizard of Oz* in layman's terms that would be helpful to both adults and children."

I was asked if we could agree on a deadline of two weeks. My mind was racing and I found myself beginning to write the piece in my head there and then. In my excitement and nervousness I felt I had come home.

"Yes, that should be fine," I heard myself say. Inside I was thinking *I hope so, gulp!* I could see my mum's face. MGM—she would not have believed it. My dad, who had died many years before her, would have been stunned that 'the mug' (cockney term for idiot) as he often called me, had made it!

I was sent a copy of *The Wizard of Oz* to work from, and started to make notes whenever the inspiration hit me. My daughter Claire kindly deciphered and typed up my writing from the backs of receipts, other bits of paper or whatever was to hand when ideas occurred. (I am in fact writing this at the counter of the Halifax Building Society while I wait for receipts for cheques I have just paid in. Such is the kind of creative chaos my family has to deal with. *Love 'em!*)

The phone rang.

"Hello, Bernie. MGM love it. They want you to do an interview with Vanessa Feltz on the Channel 4 programme *The Big Breakfast* tomorrow morning at 5am." So began a series of TV and radio, interviews and programmes—including twenty two radio interviews in one day alone. My life changed significantly from that moment.

When the alarm clock woke me at 4am I peered out of the window to see it was still dark and snowing, and wanted to go back to bed. I remembered I was going to *The Big Breakfast* studio for my first television appearance with Vanessa Feltz, live. Now I really wanted to go back to bed!

There was a knock on my door.

"Morning! I'm Bill, your driver for *The Big Breakfast*."

"Hello, Bill. Ok, I'm ready."

We got into a beautiful black car with a dashboard like a Boeing 747. The music was on softly, it was warm inside, and there was smell of leather and newness. When I closed the car door it made that low thump of a sound that left me cocooned in security, cut off from the world. As we chatted Bill told me about his job.

"I had Swampy (the eco-warrior) in here the other night and his girlfriend. Nice bloke, whiffed a bit, but nice. He told me how he used to have a sign writing business in this area."

We arrived at a business park in Stratford, London. It was still dark, sleet steadily falling. Bill directed me to a portocabin where a woman called Patsy greeted me and slapped a white circular disc on my right lapel which read 'The Movie Therapist'. I felt as if I was going on TV with Dame Edna Everage who says, "Pass the badge, Madge".

I sat waiting with a group of other participants, taking in the surreal scene in front of me. Here I was in London, and there was a man dressed as a court jester with bells on his hat jingling every time that he moved. He looked so fed up that I wondered *Who's he going to cheer up?* That thought, and looking at him, made me laugh. *Bernie boy,* I thought, *this is show business! What are you doing here?*

As I mused I looked out of the window to see what looked like a custom-built milk chocolate coloured Jaguar drive in. A woman got out in full evening dress. It was my first glimpse of Vanessa Feltz.

"Can you come through please?"

We were now in the studio behind the camera. Presenters Johnny Vaughan and Denise Van Outen were doing their knockabout—there was such great chemistry between them.

I was standing in a line. A couple of people from an up-and-coming pop group were there, laughing and joking nervously. Then I looked up from my 5ft 2inch position. Next to me was a 6ft Egyptian mummy, swathed head to foot in bandages, with a square cut out so you could see his face. He looked more fed up than the court jester. He looked down at me and said glumly, "Hello mate."

"Hello," I replied as though there was nothing unusual about this situation. I could hear the jester bells behind but couldn't see him. I so enjoyed the craziness of it all. I then noticed that the identity sticker on the mummy said 'Mummy'— well, what else could he possibly be!

Vanessa talked very loudly. I was guided to an armchair on her right. She sort of looked at me side on and boomed, "Movie Therapy, what's that?" She grimaced like she had just eaten a raw lemon. As I saw the 'lemon look' on Vanessa's face, a real sense of panic went through me. This was my first ever television appearance and it was live. I had no idea what questions she was going to ask; and in the event they revealed in no way a full understanding of what I actually did. She set the agenda while I was boxed into a corner of merely answering.

Her questions were based on mistaken assumptions about the way I worked; but in a two-minute interview there was no time for me to elaborate, as I had to keep up with the pace and progression of her next questions. An example of this was when she said something along the lines of, "This is a very unorthodox form of therapy. One film you often use is *The Wizard of Oz*. Here is a clip from it—why would you show them this?"

The assumption was that I normally showed and prescribed films for people; I had no time to explain that I use a multiplicity of films with a given client where it is helpful and appropriate. Vanessa would also cut me off in mid-answer, missing out the most vital point. As I glanced up at the Mummy towards the end, even he was looking nervous. But I had done it!

Finally I was asked by Vanessa what was my favourite film. I said, *It's A Wonderful Life*. Afterwards I was reproached by the PR company representing MGM who wanted to know why I hadn't promoted *The Wizard of Oz* as my favourite film. I responded that this had been a personal question put to me and I had answered it honestly.

At the end of the interview I remembered how the previous year I had been asked to go on *The Big Breakfast* to be interviewed by Zig and Zag (two puppets who appeared daily on the show at that time!). I suddenly knew that my decision not to accept that interview had certainly been the right one!

The really nice surprise came at the end of the show when all the guests were invited to tuck into a huge free big breakfast. It was a delicious fry up of beans, eggs, bacon, mushrooms, tomatoes, sausages, chips, coffee and toast.

I got home to find the telephone ringing. It was this radio show, that radio show, this magazine, that magazine. Producers and programmes feed off each other's coverage so I ended up doing many more media interviews than the ones originally set up for me via MGM.

It was exciting, frightening and stimulating all at the same time—an emotional learning curve and something of a roller coaster for me. But that was how my work on movie therapy came to attract a lot of public attention and why it continues to do so.

I include here an account of my appearance on the BBC television programme *Here And Now*. They wanted me to do movie therapy with a woman who had a phobia about birds. I declined but surprisingly, almost once a fortnight, the director persisted with the invitation, saying he would ensure it would be a fair presentation of what I do. I finally agreed, and they took me to a small cinema in Soho Square. There I was shown a short clip of the woman who had been taken to Trafalgar Square, to illustrate her response to the pigeons. Later that day I was introduced to her, to see if we could work together. It was agreed that we would start filming the next day, in an old building that had once been a church in Harlesden. It was on and off for three days. The woman's film, was *The Birdman of Alcatraz*, and they'd had the ingenious idea of using blue screen technology to make us both part of the film—appearing alongside Burt Lancaster in the chaotic scene where he is surrounded by birds.

The programme's format was to show viewers what happened and then to interview the lady about her experience of movie therapy, leaving viewers to make up their own minds about its credibility. The challenge was in doing live therapy and remaining focused and authentic, whilst having to let go of the complex conditions I was having to work in. Therapy traditionally takes place in a quiet room, as a relationship between client and therapist. Here it was whole new ball game, with the distracting factors of heat from the camera lights, the need to hit your marks for the camera precision, and the vision of the director.

Therapeutic relationships, like any relationship, take time to develop and grow; but here I found myself in a unique situation in which I'd met the woman only an hour before, yet we were required to do switch into therapy mode, with all the demands and complexity, that live filming requires.

However all the way through this, I felt intuitively that something was not right, but could not put my finger on it. After all the false starts, timing issues and not hitting the marks as required, we completed the piece. In the finished programme the scene was shown to the viewers, and then the woman was interviewed about her experience of movie therapy. She said I had helped her, but she wasn't sure if it was me and not the film. I was a little disappointed but also pleased. Nicky Campbell just looked into the camera with a quizzical look, and it was left to the viewers to decide.

A few days after the programme was shown, I had a phonecall. To my surprise, it was the woman with the phobia with whom I had worked on the show. She said how much I had helped her and that it was becoming more evident now she was back home.

"I feel guilty, Bernie," she confessed. "There's something I have to tell you."

What could that be? I wondered, fascinated. She explained that the film used, *The Birdman of Alcatraz*, was not her film.

"My film, and what really affected me, was actually the Alfred Hitchcock film *The Birds*."

My intuition clicked. So that's what was wrong.

"Don't worry," I said, "but thank you. Because what you've told me is very helpful for me to know."

This confirmed that it had to be, not any old film simply because it had birds in it, but the right film and the right moment in it. As I said earlier, you have no control and in this case, not all the knowledge and facts. She said, "*The Birds* was too expensive for the TV company to pay for the clip, but because

The Birdman of Alcatraz was part of a promotional offer by the film company, looking to promote a re-release, it was cheaper."

It was at that moment, I decided to write a book to clarify, what movie therapy is and what it isn't.

I include here a proposal I made to MGM:

CHITTY CHITTY BANG BANG:
MEDIA PUBLICITY PROPOSAL

Thank you for inviting me to contribute my ideas for maximising the PR for Chitty Chitty Bang Bang (CCBB). Time is short so I will fax you this letter today: the original will follow by post.

CCBB exists as a story by Ian Fleming, the inventor of James Bond, and as a film which you are re-releasing on video. My approach is designed to target the huge existing Bond audience as a new market for a video re-release.

I believe MGM could achieve excellent coverage by promoting three aspects of the re-release together: the author of the story, the film itself, and topical therapeutic angles. I'd like to help MGM capitalise on all these, and my concepts are outlined below:

THE STORY THAT JAMES BOND TOLD HIS CHILDREN

CCBB reveals much about the values that Ian Fleming wanted to pass on. The same themes and values are, to a great extent, present in all the James Bond stories. You might want to consider a feature that puts Ian Fleming in the psychiatrist's chair, looking at what he was seeking to communicate in his story and why, by making comparisons between CCBB and later Bond novels.

- Fleming wrote the story for his 7 year old son when he was recovering in a clinic from heart attack.
- He is quoted as saying that his James Bond stories were fairytales for adults.
- His own inventive character was brought to life, in the Inventor, Commander Potts, who was later transformed into Q in the Bond stories.
- A friend's daughter, Jemima Pitman, was the model for Jemima Potts.
- Truly Scrumptious is recognisable throughout the Bond era as Miss Moneypenny.
- CCBB is the car that drives in water (and flies) in the Bond movies.

- Fleming asked Trog, the Daily Mail cartoonist, to illustrate the book. But this was allegedly vetoed by the Daily Mail because Ian Fleming was a correspondent for the rival Daily Express. Do you think the Express might be interested in an exclusive? If so, I'd be happy to talk to my contacts there on your authority.
- The script for the film was started by Roald Dahl (a fellow intelligence officer), but Dahl was sacked for being too slow.
- Fleming's life and output, and the light this throws on the CCBB story, would make a fascinating and intellectually stimulating feature. If you think MGM would like to arrange an interview with me on this angle, I would be happy to contribute to the feature.

22 A MEETING
OF MINDS

I received a call one day from a Scottish woman running a media course at Leeds Trinity University. She introduced herself as Maggie Roux and asked, "Would you be interested in giving a lecture to my students, as I find your work fascinating?"

It was a great honour to be asked to lecture at a university—something I had never done before—and I felt very pleased. By then I had taken part in lots of television and radio shows, yet funnily enough the thought of standing in front of a group of people in an academic setting made me nervous. I said I was interested so we discussed a fee and made arrangements. The lecture was to be titled Reel Feelings. As we talked it became clear that those attending would be social workers, hospice workers, media workers, retreat directors and students.

Maggie then went on to tell me about the synchronicity of reading about me in a Daily Express article published a year earlier. She had meant to ring then, but had lost the article with my number on it, only finding it almost a year and a day later.

All was set and I arranged to meet her. As we had agreed in advance on the films we would talk about, Maggie had them all ready when I got there. Small, sparkly eyed and dynamic, with a great knowledge of her subjects, Maggie greeted me in a very warm and friendly way. Such was her enthusiasm that simply being with her gave you energy. Her sharp mind relentlessly roamed her huge expanses of knowledge like those huge plains so marvellously shown in the film *Dances with Wolves*.

The course run by Maggie was very successful and she invited me to come again. She also introduced me to Peter Malone, president of *Signis,* the international catholic organisation for cinema, and film critic for the Catholic Church.

Maggie had arranged for Peter to meet us outside the British Museum. It was a lovely warm day and Maggie walked up to him to greet him with a kiss.

"Peter, this is Bernie." We both smiled. He had a greyish beard, kind smiling eyes and spoke softly with an unmistakable Australian accent.

"I've been reading about you in the *St Trope*," he said in a complimentary way that put me at my ease. "I don't agree with you about the film *I'll Never Forget What's His Name.*"

I was surprised at this and warmed to Peter immediately. He was referring to a comment I had made in an article—that I had never met anyone who knew what that film was about. For me it just summed up the films of the 60s/70s era that weren't to my liking at all.

"Shall we go in here?" Maggie asked, motioning to a little pub. I glanced at the lovely cold pints on the pavement tables.

"Yes, we can sit out here," I said. Peter was still eyeing me with friendly interest, getting a sense of what I was like. I was feeling good about our shared love of film; and Maggie was very pleased with how well we got on. That was the start of a three and a half hour discussion on films, lines from films, the meaning of films, and therapy. It was a fascinating and creative meeting of minds on a sunny, breezy day, with the bustle of tourists visiting the museum. It was one of those moments you never forget and when it's very, very good to be alive.

I know very little about the Catholic Church and was surprised to see Peter in ordinary clothes without a dog collar. I would never have known he was a priest. His everyday life was interviewing directors such as Peter Yates and Steven Spielberg. He wrote critical reviews for the catholic press and had a phenomenal memory for films, dates of reviews, stars and directors.

The time seemed to fly, and the seeds were sown for a joint book on the therapeutic value of film by Maggie, Peter and myself, plus another seminar at Leeds Trinity University.

The second conference at the university was a much bigger affair than my first lecture, running for three days. It took place in one of those lecture rooms that is laid out in the round, so you are lower than members of the audience who look down to the centre.

There was no rehearsal: we just went straight into it. Maggie gave the introduction based on her amazing knowledge of film. The great thing was that Peter or I could come in at any time if we wanted to make a specific point. Those attending could also register that they wanted to ask a question. Somehow it all worked without a hitch.

Interestingly, there was in the audience a Benedictine monk called Mark—highly intelligent, intellectual and very articulate. He told me he had a strong reaction against the film *It's a Wonderful Life* as he felt he was being manipulated. I just asked him, "Could you drop your intellectual analysis of the film and feel the feelings of the film so you can really get its message?"

I also said gently, "I wonder if your intellectual approval is something you use as a defence against feelings?" This had quite an impact on Mark. I ended by discussing with people in a group about their chosen films and the feelings that they raised.

The conference was a huge success and a great learning curve for me. In their feedback sheets, most of the participants said they had found it excellent and could not wait for the next one. I felt incredibly happy and very grateful to Maggie and Peter for inviting me to participate in the seminars. I discovered how much I actually knew, and sometimes had to pinch myself to make sure I wasn't dreaming—that I was actually lecturing in a university.

The experience gave me more confidence, and in many ways I felt like I had come home. It felt so right to be there, doing what I was doing. Maggie was thrilled and excited. She was already making ambitious plans, including tours of the US and Canada, and it was a joy to experience her enthusiasm and dynamism. The practicalities of how we would do it all seemed irrelevant: we were just enjoying the moment.

On the train back I replayed in my mind the whole three-day experience, thinking about how much I had learned, how I would do it differently again, and the sheer pleasure of being exposed to Peter and Maggie's huge knowledge of their subjects.

It was also very interesting for Peter and Maggie meeting and talking to me as a Buddhist psychotherapist. So we were learning from each other and, I suppose you could say, bonding at a kind of interfaith level. The conference had also marked the start of a long working relationship between Mark, the Benedictine monk, and myself. This is what Mark wrote later in response to my request for feedback after the conference:

WORKING WITH BERNIE

The word "synchronicity" is going to force its way into anything I attempt to write about Bernie, so I take synchronicity as the place to begin. 'When the disciple is ready, the guru will appear,' says an old Indian proverb. Doubtless, Bernie would reject the term "guru" as applied to himself, but the proverb communicates exactly my sense of the timeliness of his appearances in my own life.

When I first met Bernie, at a conference on film and personal development, his directness and simplicity of approach to a subject matter I always tend to overcomplicate took me by surprise. He is a man who communicates at a very straightforwardly personal level, gentle, receptive – and so strongly grounded that you feel it wouldn't be possible to push him over. It is as if his energy flows from deep down, almost from the earth beneath his feet. As someone who is always inclined to fly off into airy nothings, I found that Bernie's presence as much as what he said was a lesson in being there, in settling into oneself. It came as a timely gift, at a moment when I needed the strength to settle into some difficult recognitions of my own, this willingness to listen and ability to hear what is really being said, even when one doesn't recognise it oneself.

On more than one occasion since that first meeting, I've benefited from Bernie's extraordinary sixth sense of when it might be wise to pick up the phone. How does he do it? Search me! But he generally manages to choose a moment when his calm conversation is exactly the tonic needed to restore a lost perspective or open up a new vista on something that appears problematic.

Perhaps most importantly, he has the great gift of being completely unselfish in his dealings with others. He demonstrates the skill of setting others free, not binding to himself those with whom he spends his time.

Why haven't I mentioned film? Perhaps because I'm never really conscious of Bernie "using" film as a technique in his dealings with me. Curious, really, but perhaps rightly so. The best special effects don't draw attention to themselves, they serve the narrative or character development of the story in which they feature.

Similarly, Bernie moves easily from personal experience to spiritual insight, through a Hollywood moment or two, and back to something that happened in the family. He hasn't said this to me, but I suspect that he would suggest the way he reflects with his clients and others on the role film plays in our lives is a paradigm for all sensitive reflection on experience. Perhaps, like dreams, film is a privileged ideogram of the soul, but my sense is that for Bernie it is the soul that matters, not the film.

23 THERAPY AND CATHOLICISM

I entered a period of trying to adjust my perceptions of Catholicism and Catholics to a new reality. A number of my clients included lapsed Catholics who did not talk glowingly of growing up with nuns and priests. Many of them had understood and experienced a great deal of harshness from convents and monasteries and an old doctrine of Catholicism that for them was no longer viable.

I took advantage of my new collaboration with Maggie Roux and Peter Malone to ask them about Catholicism and deepen my knowledge of it. I asked for their advice in helping my clients who had been brought up as Catholics; I also took healing and spiritual advice from Peter as a priest speaking on behalf of the church today.

One of my lapsed Catholic clients, a woman of great experience, wrote at my request about her relationship with the church. It underlined for me the power of the inner critic in people which, in her case and in the case of many Catholics, has been even more reinforced by the power of the church:

HAVING BEEN A CATHOLIC ONCE, TWICE, NEVER AGAIN

The title is an allusion to my inability to free myself from the
ties of the church: I left for some years as a student, returning

for my marriage and for my children, and have now not practised for about six years.

Although I have great feeling for the compassion there is within the Catholic Church and I am personally drawn to the light that is Christ, I have chosen to part company from the confines within which I was brought up. (I would be pretty unlikely now to join any established church.)

'Confining' is a very lukewarm kind of word for how I feel about my Catholic upbringing: it was suppressive to the point of extinction—only now, age 57, and just in time, am I regaining strength and individuality and confidence enough to discover my true being. Whether well meant or not is immaterial: my individuality was systematically squashed and demolished and the subsequent bewilderment has led to desperate trouble. No life is free of pain, of difficulty—but this?

A steely, suffocating, cruel and heartless hierarchical regime built on guilt and fear was played out at my home, albeit through lack of perception—for there was love. And this regime was exacerbated at school about 200%. These are strong words, but this is how I feel and I can give plenty of examples.

Even now, if I come across Catholics, although there is much kindness, much compassion, there are those whom I cannot trust, beneath whose smiling faces there are steely, power-seeking fingers—the tips of which stroke and purr and manipulate.

I did not want this for my children either but such was my fear for my son's well-being that I did have my first baptised at four months. Some of the time during his childhood I resisted having to follow the dictates of the church, but eventually succumbed from the direct, indirect and internal pressures I felt, all emanating one way or another from the Catholic Church. At the age of 11 my eldest child needed to make his first communion in order to attend a catholic secondary school, so at this time I finally had my 7 year-old twins baptised.

I shall never forget how I felt one day when they were in their first year—angry, guilty, and bewildered. We were visiting my aunt who was then an enclosed Carmelite. There were these two little dots, completely innocent, and yet I was left in no uncertainty as to the 'poverty' of their un-baptised state. I was urged to clear up this deficiency in their lives with all speed, clearly being told that I was letting them down.

I fail to see how such innocents can have come from a place of such darkness, how they could be tainted, how they would have returned to a place of semi-darkness reserved for the un-baptised had they died in this state. As far as I was and am concerned they had come from the light and we were the ones who were privileged to be in their presence. (I think I could tolerate baptism more in all the Christian Churches if, maybe, it was seen as a protection against the dangers of the world and a real support to getting through life.)

I find as I begin to realise more and more fully the extent of my dumbing down, seeing that a good deal more than half of my life has been subject to the actuality or residue of such manipulative, insensitive and cruel activities of the Catholic

Church, it would be easy to become bitter. Sometimes I am. Certainly, I shall never trust it again, and I hugely resent being called a 'lapsed' or 'resting' Catholic as if my humanity, my being, can only be whole and true if I return to the church.

I am interested in the leaders such as Christ, Buddha and Mohammed and in the free discovery of truth and freedom that is un-prescriptive, and I feel that unless the church becomes wider and accepts the spirituality of all of us, with no ulterior motive such as hoping that loosening the reins will bring people back, my feelings will remain the same.

Finally, I am angered by the fact that as a woman I would be disallowed from being a priest, should I wish. My gender may colour the way I view life, how I react etc. but it is complete nonsense to state I have the wrong qualities, experiences and capabilities to be a spiritual leader in this way.

I think that the negative inner critic that many people have is compounded, in the case of Catholics, by the authority, majesty and power of the church. I have seen how this can have a very adverse effect. Those of my clients who are lapsed Catholics often feel judged to be bad in a spiritual way. While I am sure there are many millions of Catholics around the world who have not had this experience, those I have worked with are struggling with fear, criticism, harshness and cruelty.

I have also found that figures in churches frightened many of my Catholic clients. One of them remains frightened to this day of any kind of statue or mannequin, because of the associated wounds that she suffered as a young girl—a trauma we are beginning to deal with in therapy now.

24 STORIES ALONG THE WAY

One day when I'd taken my wife to a hospital appointment I suddenly realised time was getting on, so I told her, "I must get back for my client at 3pm. I'll see you at home." We said goodbye and I went to catch the train from Farringdon.

I arrived home with about ten minutes to spare and felt relieved. Then—I could not believe it—I had no door key. This is not something that happens to me, as I'm so careful and take my responsibilities very seriously. Now there were only five minutes until the client was due to arrive. What could I do? I thought of the garden, wondering if it was too public. Then I realised my garden was very private and secure and there was no one about at that time of the day, so I thought it should feel safe for the client. If she was not happy with this arrangement we could reschedule for another day.

The client loved the idea—the novelty, and the change: it suited her personality and the work we were doing in her therapy. It could all be used creatively and, as she was a jazz singer, improvisation was very important to her.

What was also revealing was my client's response when I later asked if she would give me permission to mention our session in the garden in this book. She said, "You'll have to remind me, I really don't remember. I could have our sessions almost anywhere within reason so long as the place was not too public. Where we go together is so important, so strong."

So I asked, "You feel safe?"

"Oh yes," she said. It was a clear indication of our healthy relationship. I was pleased: it showed the extent to which a therapist can indulge in professional satisfaction. I believe the relationship between therapist and client is the main factor in healing. John C Norcross also found this in his own research.

Unknown to me however, my wife had returned home not long after our session started. Seeing us in the garden she'd thought, "Oh that's nice. They're doing the session in the sun—I suppose it makes a change."

After the client left by the garden gate, I looked up casually, wondering how long my wife would be, so I could get in. To my surprise I saw her wave to me through the net curtains and then she was gone! I walked up to the patio door but still couldn't get in. I was by this point very hot, very dry and completely bemused by my wife's behaviour.

So I decided to walk round to my front door and knock. My wife came to the door, looked surprised and said, "What are you doing here?' Even more surprised, I replied, probably with a hint of sarcasm, "I live here!"

"Yes," said my wife laughing, "but why didn't you come through the patio door?"

"Because it's still locked," I said. We then stood and just looked at each other in confusion. Gradually we became more amused as it dawned on us what had happened. I explained, "You still have my front door key and I couldn't get in. Which is why I had to do the session in the garden."

My wife thought this was terrifically funny.

"Oh," she managed between laughing, "I thought you wanted a change in the sun!" Now she was doubled up at the thought of her earlier wave to me through the net curtains and how my sense of relief at seeing her was so short lived as she vanished.

There is something very 'Goldie Hawn' about my wife. When I said, "I'm parched, can I have a cup of tea?" she replied with a straight face but just a hint of humour, "Where do you want it, in the garden?" and burst out laughing again.

It was yet another therapeutic spin-off for me from working with a client.

I SMOKE SITTING BULL'S PIPE

I had an offer I just couldn't refuse. A friend rang and said, "Bernie! Would you like to smoke Sitting Bull's pipe?"

Unsure of whether I was victim of a practical joke, I said, "What, the real one?"

"The real one," he answered, and I heard him laughing on the end of the phone. "Come down at 7.30 tomorrow"

I said, "Ok," still feeling it was some practical joke.

I arrived at 7.30 the next evening and was intoduced to a professor of antiquities, and his wife. He was dressed in jeans and jacket; his wife was dressed as a squaw!

We sat round in a circle while they burnt some sage; the professor told us a story of how he had spent years helping the Sioux tribe to establich their rights to their land in the Black Hills of Dakota. In gratitude for this the Sioux had bestowed on him the great honour and weighty responsibility of being the next keeper of Sitting Bull's pipe. The pipe had previously been passed on only to members of the tribe; but they had made an exception and handed over the pipe to the professor's safe keeping.

As we sat in the circle, the professor picked up an object wrapped in buckskin and slowly opened it. It was the pipe, and it was striking: approximately three feet long and made of red sandstone. The sense of history in it was fascinating, when you recalled the important role it had played in early American Indian history.

The professor filled the pipe with sage, took a puff and, in the traditional manner, handed to the next of us to his left. When it reached me I was amazed at the weight of it. I puffed at the sage smoke, and found it had no noticeable effect on me; but I did observe that, as it went round the circle, the atmosphere had a sacred feel. I wasn't expecting this.

Later the professor told us two unusual stories about the tribes helping him. He had been informed by one of the elders that spiders would protect him; and so if he saw one, he should take it as a warning. The professor was quietly amused, but listened respectfully.

Some months later he was driving through the mountains at two o'clock in the morning, in torrential rain. Suddenly he heard a clicking noise. He looked round and saw two spiders in the left corner of the car. The earlier warning flashed across his mind, and he slowed right down as he came to the next bend. The road in front was strewn with car wreckage and boulders. Ambulances were tending the injured drivers. This was a story not of his belief but from his experience: but it did make him think.

His next experience, a year later, made him think much more. He bacame very ill and was taken into hospital, where the doctors were very concerned about him. One evening three Sioux elders came to visit him. They did a quiet ceremony around him, murmuring incantations and burning sage. He recounted that he'd felt very hot and had then drifted off to sleep. When he awoke there was a feather on his pillow and, to his surprise, he felt much stronger.

When his doctor arrived on his rounds, he was confounded, and immediately ordered tests. He could not believe the professor's amazing recovery, but kept him in hospital for a further night in case of a relapse. But there was none, and he left the next day.

But it does make you think: as with many indigenous tribes throughout the world, they know much that we do not.

MY AA EXPERIENCE

One day I was watching an advertisement for the Automobile Association on television when a whole business concept came to me that I thought was highly original. It was in two parts. In the advert they concentrated on the car and the breakdown; but I thought it was the AA member who was important, rather than the car.

It seemed to me that the way the AA could demonstrate that to their millions of members was to offer the option of counselling after certain kinds of accident. I could not understand how no one had thought of it before, so I called the AA head office and asked to speak to their public relations people. I was passed onto Matthew Joint, their psychologist. I said I felt that if they went with the idea that the person was the member rather than the car, the member would feel safe in the knowledge that the AA was looking after them even further by offering counselling in the aftermath of an accident. My company could provide such a service.

I was very pleased with the response. Matthew Joint, a most agreeable man, thought it was a very good idea, asked pertinent questions and said he would get back to me. I was amazed how quickly a meeting was arranged with three top managers to discuss my proposal.

In tandem with this meeting I was interviewed by a man called John Murray whose business supplied counsellors to firms to help their employees. Firms who wanted to hold onto the employees' particular skills would offer them counselling as an extension of the human resources department. The firm would pay for six sessions, on a purely confidential basis, for each employee.

John Murray was a big hearty man, Australian, around 6'3". He was very friendly but firm too: he had great authority. Whilst he was interviewing me my mind kept being drawn for some reason to an antique table to my right and my thoughts were of monks.

As always, I went with my intuition and decided to mention it.

"John, I don't know why I am thinking about this, but I just feel it necessary to tell you that I am thinking about the table and monks—I feel I am picking up something."

John just smiled in an understanding way, never missed a beat, and carried on with the interview. To my surprise at the end of the interview he said, "I definitely want to employ you, but I want you for *executive mentoring.*" This was the first time I had heard the term. "I would still like you for counselling," he continued, "but for executive mentoring as well: you will be excellent for it."

He gave as an example of executive mentoring a highly pressured executive who flies into town and stays at a hotel for one or two nights. Business people, he suggested, may need to be brought down to earth gently by someone who can go to their intellectual level but at the same time is earthed and has the necessary maturity, authority and gravitas to spend a couple of hours helping to calm them. Many business people in this situation begin to drink too much, but the mentoring helps them to relax.

At the end John said one of the reasons he wanted to hire me was my accuracy in something I had mentioned earlier. He said the table I had mentioned was a monks' writing table and seat. By pulling a lever on the side you could turn the bale into the seat. The table then came up and became the back of the seat. It was a design that involved no metal, just wood.

John continued, "I am very impressed that you picked that up, as I was a monk for 15 years in Australia." We bonded very quickly at quite a deep level, having much to talk about as John was a Roman Catholic and I a Buddhist.

After that interview we stayed in touch. I left the Hammersmith river boat on the Thames where he had his business. Then I met my wife who was waiting for me in a nearby restaurant and went to see the musical *River Dance* which we thoroughly enjoyed.

The AA were very keen and wanted to set a date for me to meet them, sooner rather than later. I finally agreed a date even though I didn't as yet have a business set up to take on a contract. Then it occurred to me to ask John to join me in this venture. It was my idea, contact and set up, but he had the necessary business and counsellors in place. If he could agree we would be up and running.

I had a meeting with John where he jumped at my idea with customary enthusiasm. So a meeting was set up and John and I went to see Mathew Joint and the AA management and public relations executives at their Basingstoke headquarters. When we got to the meeting I ran through the idea. The PR people were very excited but the accountant looked worried, as all accountants do when it comes to spending money—that is their job after all.

My final gambit as I put the idea to them was that it was not a case of *if* a motoring organisation would offer this but rather *when*, and who would have the competitive edge. That seemed really to get them focused. Meanwhile the accountant was looking even more unhappy as the sense of urgency had been brought to the proceedings and he had no costings.

These meetings went on and off for a year, with costings being put forward together with pilot schemes. Unfortunately, however, the AA was taken over by Centrica and much of their executive management changed, so in the end there was no agreement.

Matthew Joint remained very enthusiastic about the scheme. We stayed in touch and he occasionally referred AA members to me who had experienced the trauma of an accident and were now too nervous to drive. He also mentioned my name on Virgin Radio, suggesting that people should call me if they had been involved in an accident or a road rage incident.

It was a great shame that the AA could not have set up a pilot in an area and run with it. Still, the idea may come to fruition one day.

THERAPISTS FOR VOICE MOVEMENT

This was an amazing experience of group therapy. Therapists for Voice Movement consisted of opera singers, actors, actresses and therapists—with lots of explosive temperament!

My role was to work with any transference that came up from individual trainees around director and trainer Paul Newham. The objective was to neutralise, as much as possible, any of the negative emotional transference, so that the tutorial would go much more smoothly and the trainee would be much more receptive to Paul's knowledge. Paul was an interesting and charismatic man, an innovator and an expert on the voice. He was in many ways a natural therapist and could have been a therapist or a director. The latter had a stronger pull on him and eventually won out, which was a great shame.

I first attended a week's training as a participant and it proved to be an extraordinary week. One day in particular stands out. It involved an exercise where every one of the seventeen participants had to make their own *sound*. We had to make a sound that came from the deepest part of us, whatever that sound was.

I remember it as vividly today as I did then. It was a cacophony of laughter, screams, shouts, wails, moans, lamenting and chattering, like one great 'transpersonal' opera of the human condition. The collective unconscious was made flesh in a real tangible form.

A huge wave of compassion rose up in me as I listened to us all baring our souls. With it came the realisation that all this happiness and despair lies below the surface in everyone, people in the streets, people shopping, people going about their day. We all knew it and it was somehow familiar. It was an experience of oneness yet we had never heard it before. Extraordinary!

25 WORKING VIA THE WEB

JOHN'S STORY

People look at my website and send me some fascinating stories. John was a wonderful example of this. He first contacted me by filling in a form on my website about how the film *The Third Man* had affected his life.

Although John was not a client I was intrigued by his story as revealed on his form, and we made contact. This is where a very interesting journey began for both John and me as we talked about his film and then subsequent films. I would ask him questions to help him to reveal more of himself.

John's story would, in fact, make a good film in itself. We worked together via the internet and by telephone and it was not long before I was able to give him some observations and suggestions which he found helpful. For example I asked if he had observed that Holly Martins in *The Third Man* was picking women who were unavailable and I suggested it might be helpful for him to focus on this pattern that appeared to be present in his own life.

In these extracts from his emails sent after our phone calls John explains this process in his own words...

Hello Bernie

I was a child when I saw a film that totally captivated me and has never left my mind. I have since seen it many, many times and never tire of it. It was The Third Man.

It made me realise how important films are as a medium that go even beyond their entertainment value by reaching one at a very deep psychological level. It really was the one film that hooked me on films forever. Films had always been for me a means of escaping into a fantasy world. The Third Man *was released in 1949 after our country had been at war and although the film was about the effects of one man's black market profiteering at the expense of other peoples' lives, it contained the element of magic in its memorable scenes, dialogue, and music.*

I can relate to Holly Martins, a man who seeks out a friend only to fall in love with his girl, and to lose them both in the end. And Harry Lime was, for me, a lovable rogue; never all bad, as no one ever is.

I was about 10 years of age when I saw The Third Man. *It was the first movie to educate me to what life was really all about, and started an unending love affair for me with movies.'*

'*Hello Bernie*

Thank you for the insight you have given me regarding this film, particularly relating to the repeated pattern in my life: falling in love with women who are already in a relationship—married or unable to return my love. My sympathy with Holly Martins, played by Joseph Cotton in the film, was because he loved a woman who was still in love with his friend, Harry Lime. I could recognise this pattern of unrequited love in my mother's life, and even subconsciously in my own.

What I now see is that to break this recurring theme in my love life, I need to take the plunge and realise these relationships. Also, by living my life and not the life pattern of my mother, I am able to seek partners who are free to love.

Thank you for spotlighting the reasons for my obsession with The Third Man *and also referring to the* The Bridges of Madison County *and* Letter from an Unknown Woman *which were relevant to my case.'*

'Hello Bernie

I have just viewed the video of Letter from an Unknown Woman, *a film recommended by you regarding the similarity between the main character in the film and that of my mother.*

In the film, Louis Jourdan's character receives a letter from a woman who claims that she had been in love with him many years ago. She says that love had been rekindled when they met some years later—but unfortunately he could not remember her. Jourdan reads the letter after the woman, played by Joan Fontaine, has died.

My mother always regretted not marrying an army officer who was stationed in India. She never forgot him. Some years later, with the full knowledge of my father, she had written to a woman whom she believed once knew him. The letter was returned to her with a brief message that she did not remember anyone by that name.

When I was a child, my mother would tell me about this man and even showed me a photograph of him. She never stopped wondering what would have happened if she had gone to India and married 'Johnnie'.

Seeing the film brought this all back to me—lost love. In my own love life I have followed a paradigm of somehow always falling in love with women who are 'not available,' either because they are already married or are too young. It is as though I am subconsciously sabotaging my love life by choosing impossible relationships. As you have pointed out, to break this pattern I need to examine why I am doing this. Perhaps I am preventing myself from finding my true love by deliberately saving myself, and being there, for my mother.

Seeing this film, and also The Third Man, *allowed me to be the observer to characters that I could recognise as myself or my mother. I could feel the loss, the sadness, the incredible knowing that I was writing my own unhappy ending.*

I have since been able to address this life-long problem, thanks to you, Bernie, and am now looking forward to sealing a beautiful loving relationship without fear.'

'Hello Bernie

Your comments about my reactions to The Bridges of Madison County *allowed me to take another look at my relationship with my father. You may recall that I said that*

I sympathised more with Meryl Streep's character in the film than that of Clint Eastwood's. You suggested that I examine why my mother played such an important part in my life and also why I had reduced my father's role to that of a supporting player (my words, not yours). You advised me to look at my father's life with new eyes, almost like rediscovering him and in so doing, maybe giving him back the hero status that I had denied him.

Well, I have taken your advice and was quite surprised to find a 'new dad'. Rummaging through old family photographs and brushing away the cobwebs in my mind, I saw a man who failed to live up to his own expectations, who tried so hard to win respect and love, to have a better job, to be a better father and a better husband.

I think he died without realising that he had achieved success in many areas of his life. He had won the girl of his dreams and married her. He had fathered two children, my brother and me, and had brought us up in a happy, loving home.

I remember my childhood with great pleasure: they were times of fun and laughter and music. My father emerged as a man with many wonderful gifts that he allowed us to witness on occasions: the artist, the craftsman, the comedian, the poet, the musician; any of which he could have pursued as a career. I realised that the hours he spent working and making paper impressions using beeswax influenced my love of printing and art. I also learnt patience from him, a quality that he had more than anyone I have ever met or am likely to meet.

There was also a wonderful sensitivity about him, quite a rare quality in a man, a man who was never afraid to show his emotion. I remember once when he told us that he had just witnessed a boy cyclist who had been hit by a car and as he empathised more with the boy he began to cry. I was confused by his tears, too young to understand that he had imagined that the boy could have been my brother or me.

His loyalty and love for my mother was unquestionable. When she suffered a stroke that immobilised her, he immediately left his job to look after her for the rest of her life. He cooked, cleaned and totally adapted his life to caring for the woman he loved. He became a hero and he played it magnificently.

I look back at my father's life and can now truly say that I understand what he did and love him for it.

Thanks Bernie. Thanks Bridges. *Thanks Dad.*

Finally, I recall going to the cinema to see The Robe. *It was one of my dad's favourite films. I like to think that he saw the hero as himself, just as I now see the hero in him.*

Kindest regards, John'

ANNA'S STORY

Anna's case illustrates that it is not necessary for some people to be in therapy for a film to have a beneficial therapeutic effect...

'I saw The Lord of the Rings *for the first time just after Christmas 2001. I was already familiar with the works of Tolkien and had enjoyed his books. I had a chest infection at*

the time but had already bought the tickets to take my 13 year old daughter and her two friends to the cinema. I just wanted to get the visit over and go home. What I found was that I was completely spellbound by the film. The costumes, the sets and acting were impressive but it was much more than that.

It was a time in my life when I was feeling powerless. I was going through a most unpleasant divorce, my daughter had been very unwell and I was not particularly happy in my teaching post.

The film inspired me. It is about a small group of people continuing on a quest to overcome evil. I found the film more moving and inspiring than the book although I have enjoyed both.

The story is also about finding the inner strength to continue when the path we are on seems impossibly difficult. This is reflected in the words of Gandalf when Frodo is anxious and regrets what has happened to him, "so do all who have lived to see such times but that is not for them to decide, all you have to decide is what to do with the time that is given to you." The film is very much about having courage to go on, something I needed at that time.

The story is also about evil or the dark side. It helped me reflect on my own shadow and the quest for power. Power comes in different forms and disguises. There are many dark figures in my inner world put there for their power when I was a child. The shadow is a place of great creativity. The film helped me go deeper into this area.

Some of the characters also made me look at aspects in my own life. Boromir was particularly meaningful to me. He is the one who is most tempted by the ring and then to make recompense gives his life in battle. Before he dies he calls for help but it comes too late. On a personal level this took me back to when I was bullied at school and no one came to help, also being bullied by my ex-husband, and the death of my father when I arrived at the hospital too late to say goodbye to him—something I have never really got over.

The character of Frodo is also meaningful. He holds onto hope, (although at times feeling despair). He doesn't want the task that he's been given but continues to do what he believes is right, in fact he really wants to go home to the Shire and the security that holds. This has inspired me to go on although at times I felt reluctant to do so. For me this film was released at a time when I needed it.'

GALE'S STORY

Gale, who has weight problems, was devastated by the film *Shallow Hal.* In the film the character played by Gwyneth Paltrow is made up to look massively obese; but the man who is drawn to her does not see her as obese, rather as slim and attractive as Gwyneth Paltrow is in real life...

Before I went to see the film Shallow Hal *I had been worried that it might upset me. For many years I had been hugely overweight. The story is based on Gwyneth Paltrow's character being an obese person and how she is perceived by others. Although overweight, I had lived for years with the horror of the way people perceive me and treat me.*

My friend had seen the film and I asked whether she thought that it was worth me seeing it and wondered whether she thought it might upset me? She told me that it was a good film and quite funny and that it not only dealt with issues of being overweight, but others such as baldness and disabilities.

However, as I had thought, once the film got going I found myself in floods of tears—when all others were laughing hysterically. One particular scene in the film, which I don't believe many people would pick up on, is when they are at the restaurant and she breaks a chair when sitting on it. This brought back many memories to me.

There had been times when I would walk into a restaurant only to find that it was cramped with tables and I would automatically be searching for the easiest passage for me to get to a table without having to ask someone to move out of my way etc. I also hate being given a chair, which usually would be too small for me (especially when it had arm rests) and I would be too scared to relax for the duration of the meal, just in case the chair would break.

On the one hand I felt really glad that I didn't have that to worry me any longer but on the other I felt really angry with people laughing (even my friend sitting next to me) at the obese person on the screen who I so clearly identified with.

There is also a scene when the Gwyneth Paltrow character is leaving the restaurant when she hears two men walking in asking jokingly if there is any food left for them. I have had this happen to me on occasions and this really brought it all back to me.

Although the film finished on a good note by pointing out that it's not just people's looks that count I have actually experienced humiliations like those portrayed in the film for a long time. Part of me felt good, in that I don't have the verbal abuse from total strangers that I used to, but another part of me felt very angry that others can be so nasty to people all because of the way we look. I suppose it's made me see just how little self esteem I had. It also made me realise that I'm not the only one who has those feelings.'

Gale has since had the gastric band operation which makes the stomach smaller and brings about subsequent weight loss. She feels it has changed her life.

26 THE POWER OF ADVERTISING

With all the media bombarding us on a daily basis, why is it that a particular story can still stay with us? I have concluded that it is because it connects with our own personal history, triggering memories and emotions from our past. I have also found that television advertisements can have the same effect.

One client, badly abused as a child, became very upset with the advertisements of the NSPCC; they always disturbed her so much that they would make her shake and cry. She would have to leave the room until they were over because they brought back such horrific memories.

Another client by the name of Julie was very affected by an advertisement for Oxo gravy mix. When Julie came into the room you knew it. Her presence and personality immediately dominated the room. An organised, extrovert professional whose working day was divided into meetings, she had a 'golden' effect and was very glamorous. She had great mental clarity, made very quick decisions and conducted a check list in her mind of all the data she needed to make those decisions.

When Julie looked at you, you knew you had been looked at. She looked you straight in the eye, and asked pointed questions—with a frown. You got a sense of her determination and strength of character. She was quite a dynamic lady, but the wonder was that, within a few moments of arriving for our session, she would be in a heap sobbing—a side she would never have shown the world, professionally or personally.

This hidden side of Julie's character was brought out by talking about the Oxo TV advertisement, the last in a series that had been running for many years. During the advert the family is seen leaving the 'Oxo' home. They all turn and take one last look at the kitchen.

First Julie told me in a-matter-of-fact way that it made her feel a little sad, but as I gently probed, asking "How did it make you feel? Did it leave you happy or sad?" she gradually let me know what had touched her. That scene brought up the sense of loss and nostalgia for the way life was before her mum died. Therefore she was grieving for her mum and home and for that way of life.

Julie came from a very large family and was competitive because she and her siblings had to compete for attention. She had adapted into a powerful personality but that was not necessarily who she really was.

As she cried she looked like a little girl; and as she reached for the tissues, there was the discovery of how much her strong mind could keep her away from her feelings and of the problems this had created in her personal life. To think that all of this came from a short advertisement!

When a person is a strong personality and cognitive, and finds it difficult to get in touch with their feelings, advertisements and television help to speed up the course of therapy by bringing their emotions to the surface.

You can forget a thought but you do not forget an experience, so experience is a powerful thing to be used positively. Once a person has had the healing experience, all the cognitive understanding comes from that. This is the essence of how I work.

27 UNTAPPED POTENTIAL

The major DVD sales and rental company, Blockbuster, contacted me about their policy of sending 1000 videos out to British troops in Bosnia. What they specifically wanted was my seal of approval that it was therapeutic for the troops to watch films in that dangerous war zone. However I felt I could not give this unless I spoke directly to the soldiers.

I offered to go to Bosnia if they made the arrangements to fly me there and back over a long weekend. News came back from the army saying that this was possible and that they could house me in an old school. Then the whole enterprise fell through because of two main problems.

The first was that the army wouldn't pay the insurance on me; and secondly, Blockbuster was taken over by a new senior executive whose public relations philosophy for the company was totally different. It was a shame but I felt there was no way that I could *truly* say that films would help in that kind of dangerous situation where people were facing life or death situations, atrocities and post traumatic stress. My guess is that they do but I would have had to have interviewed the soldiers and their wives or partners really to know.

I could see great possibilities for the use of film, not only as an aid to army training and management debriefing, but also with others facing danger in the navy, air force, and emergency services. It was an exciting period, yet I felt there was much potential still to be realised.

I am very interested in what helps people get over post traumatic stress from war. The veterans of the Vietnam War, for instance, were helped very much by learning from Native Americans to sing together about what they had jointly experienced. Things that heal emotions and touch the soul can be, and often are, very mysterious.

The possibility of hospitals offering movies as therapy is something very close to my heart—quite understandably as I spent fourteen months in hospital as a young child. Using the time spent in hospital as an opportunity for psychological and spiritual growth as well as physical healing seems to me to be a glaring opportunity that is being missed.

Films could be shown to raise issues, provoke thought and help to prevent patients from becoming institutionalised. There could be discussions about a given issue or a person's particular problem that has been raised in a film. All of this could be programmed into the daily structure of patient management and much use could be made of hospital radio where it is available. Surely it would be possible to interview patients on air about a film that has touched them, even helped them?

Doing this could relieve patients' boredom and stress— so very therapeutically beneficial in itself—with a positive spin-off effect on their visiting loved ones. It could also lift morale, promote bonding and create more of a sense of community that could continue outside hospital once the patients leave. It could result in new friends, interests and hobbies.

It has been my experience that when you really are focused, passionate and determined about something, people come into your life who are of the same mind. For example I had a call one day from Christine Hill, who had successfully built a charity called Tommy's and who had now set up the charity Medicinema.

Medicinema, for those who don't know, was based at Guys Hospital, with the aim of building a cinema at every hospital in the country, so that long term patients in particular could get dressed and visit the cinema with their family, and have a proper afternoon out of the ward at the movies. The idea was to combat any sense of institutionalisation.

"I heard you on the radio and I am very interested in what you are doing," Christine said. "I'm involved in something similar," and she explained her aim of trying to get hospitals to have cinemas for the patients. I said I thought it was a fantastic idea and offered help with any publicity. She thanked me but said she was concentrating on fundraising for the moment.

We agreed to meet, when it became clear as we talked that our aims and objectives were very similar. The main difference was that Medicinema's priority focused on every hospital having its own cinema. But our joint aims included offering social integration and preventing institutionalisation for longer stay patients.

I was asked to attend a grand opening of a chain of movie theatres that Richard Branson had bought and had let Medicinema have the foyers, in order for them to raise money for them as a charity. There were many celebrities there, one of them being Kevin Spacey who made a speech, and said, "I am very proud to be part of this project, and impressed with the idea of movies being used therapeutically here in the UK. I only hope this spreads and catches on in America". I was obviously pleased to be part of this occasion, and with what Kevin Spacey had said. It was the brainchild of Christine Hill.

To round off the evening, we all viewed Kevin Spacey's latest film *In the Garden of Good and Evil*, and were given a free copy to take away.

I would hope that some of the new monies the government is offering to fund talking therapies within hospitals will find its way into the kind of initiatives that Christine Hill and I have been promoting.

28 THE OLD PRIEST

One wild winter's night I arrived at a monastery on the edge of the moors, having been invited to dinner there by a priest involved in a cinema organisation.

I was introduced to an old priest sitting alone at the end of the long dining table. When it was explained to him that I was a psychotherapist pioneering the use of films to help my clients he suddenly put down his knife and fork saying "I can absolutely concur with that—films do help." He explained how just one film, *One Flew Over the Cuckoo's Nest,* had enabled him to combat and unravel fifty years of being institutionalised, and to embark upon a journey of self discovery.

Watching the film, about patients in a hospital psychiatric unit, the priest had identified strongly with them. Led by Jack Nicholson's character, RP McMurphy, the patients rebel against the hospital's oppressive regime and are punished. The priest had been at first shocked, then angry, then in floods of tears, as he had seen his whole life being played out in front of him.

He said the film helped so much in breaking down his sense of being institutionalised and made him understand many of the feelings that had long troubled him. After we talked, I asked him if he would give me permission to include his story in this book, and he wrote the following:

My Life in the Light of the Film One Flew Over the Cuckoo's Nest

I had a religious upbringing and my powerful and dominant mother encouraged me to join the Junior Seminary in 1951 at the age of 11. The church had not changed for centuries and the Religious Order was a strict and regimented one.

I was a young and impressionable boy, very naive, innocent and gullible—so protected that I had no knowledge of the real world. My aim was to become a priest and my studies went well. In my holidays I had no contact with the real world. I did not even have to earn pocket money.

I was interested in the opposite sex but did not know why. I remember as a child of eight being shocked at seeing a mother breast-feeding her baby. I began to fantasise about breasts and this led to the habit of masturbation which continues to the present day. The environment I lived in was strict and ordered: no decisions had to be made, no choices or initiatives were tolerated. The best religious was the one who kept to the timetable. No contact with ordinary people was allowed, especially with the opposite sex.

Just before my ordination to the priesthood I was told that I was too immature to make a decision and my ordination was delayed. No changes were made to the environment: no help was offered to me. Finally in 1964 the attitude was "let's ordain him and hope for the best".

In 1965 I was sent to a busy working class parish. I was lost and, with an authoritarian superior, nearly had a breakdown. A year later I was moved to a rural area. It was in 1975 that the film One flew over the Cuckoo's Nest *was released. It opened up a can of worms for it seemed to take the lid off all that had gone wrong with my life.*

I saw myself as a victim of a system that had robbed me of my life and personality. I saw my insecurity as having been caused by the institution. After the film my reaction was one of anger and bitterness. I saw myself as the Jack Nicholson character, the innocent victim of an evil and unjust system. I became very unsettled and thought my best option was to leave the Order and become an ordinary secular priest. I went to a parish on the south coast but could not cope with the insecurity outside and came back after a week.

My mother died in 1979, a terrible blow which precipitated a crisis in my life. I went to a catholic psychotherapy centre for eight months. I felt my main problem was that I had never made a real commitment to celibacy and made that clear at the interview. The sad thing was that they never dealt with it or helped me to face up to it. Rather, they seemed more concerned to help me make decisions, something I still find difficult.

I took a sabbatical last year having in mind a trip across the world which I hoped might build up my self confidence. Being on my own for three months, however, did not help but made me feel even more isolated. I was invited into my present post...but I feel isolated and don't plan to stay too long.

You suggested I watch the film again, which I did. This time there was a strange twist as I did not identify with

Jack Nicholson but with Billy the shy, anxiety-ridden boy on the ward who had the stammer. You remember that Jack's character arranged for Billy to have sex with his friend's girlfriend—something that he had been afraid to ask for. The cruel end of the incident which affected me deeply was when the officials chased the girl from the room and Billy killed himself. I still wonder what it is saying to me. Is the source of my problems the fact that I can never have a girlfriend or a wife but try to console myself with religion and devotion to Mary the Mother of God? Perhaps you can throw light on my dilemma.

I said I thought he ought to take this into therapy; and though he considered coming into therapy with me, he must have decided against it as I did not hear from him again.

29 BUDDHISM, PSYCHOTHERAPY AND MOVIES

What fascinates and excites me is how we can creatively use the mind's natural ability to produce and observe our dreams. We can tap into this natural ability by using moments from films that clients have chosen and that contain for them the specific therapeutically beneficial experience. This potential for healing integration at the deepest level is to me very exciting. By surfing, if you like, the mind's established natural ability and direction, you are aligning with the already established synaptic dynamics to bring about a healing Gestalt.

The Buddhist practice of mindfulness is the core of my approach, both to life and to my work as a therapist. Mindfulness is the ability to witness thoughts, feelings and bodily sensations from a non-judgmental place, much as a mirror reflects what passes before it. It is like a silent, uninvolved witness that is just awareness.

This awareness, this witness, is outside the ego; and the development of this awareness is a very powerful tool in healing. Once experienced, it creates a powerful shift in consciousness, and the awareness that your mind is only a very small part of you is incredibly liberating.

This fundamental shift starts a de-identification with the mind ego and an increasing identification with the being. You learn to let go of your worries and not to take your anxieties so seriously, with the result that you relax more deeply into the cradling arms of being. This surrender becomes a refuge in the midst of chaos. It is energy with the quality of a healing and a calm freshness. Paradoxically, a sense of feeling alive, vibrancy and stillness are also there.

The gradual development of mindfulness allows us to witness our unconscious as old memories, old scripts, old emotions that bubble up. It takes much practice and patience to develop this awareness, this witness, but its effects are life-changing and invaluable.

I assist and support my clients in developing this witness consciousness in themselves. Movies help me to do this in a number of ways. For example, they can act as a catalyst in bringing to the conscious mind what was once unconscious and at the root of suffering—invaluable in my work with my clients.

Because films are able to get past our resistance we surrender to the experience, feeling the full impact in the moment as a scene shudders through us. We are purged of our suffering by giving full expression to it and uncovering what health lies beneath it.

Freud said the aim of psychoanalysis was to make what was unconscious conscious. Its limitations are that this operates all on the level of the ego. My aim is to replace the ego with a sense of being, peace and stillness. Film moments can produce the 'kind shock' that is needed to cut through corroding, habitual defenses and resistance, to bring peace and relief.

AKONG RINPOCHE

I went with my son for an interview with the Tibetan lama, Akong Rinpoche. When our turn came, we were ushered in to his room. Akong Rinpoche was seated, swirls of incense dancing slowly around him. He wore a gold silk robe, and his presence was very strong: so solid, so earthed, it made you feel safe. He was the rock that could take anything. His look was stern, then soft.

He was glancing at a little book. I won't go into my son's story but when Akong Rinpoche first spoke to him, the effect on him was stunning and magical. Later I told him about my cancer operation, which had left me with a colostomy bag and all the embarrassment and shame that brings. I also told him about my inability to pee normally, so that I have to self-cauterize twelve to fifteen times a day. When I am asleep at night, it is only the excruciating pain of the stomach spasms that wake me and warn me that I need to pee.

The operation had also left me sexually impotent which, of course, has its own difficulties. He looked at me sternly and said, "More compassion!" His tone felt like a rebuke, and I protested: "I'm doing my best; I have a successful psychotherapy practice, I'm as compassionate as I can be with my clients and my family." Again he intoned sternly, "More compassion, more compassion". I was surprised and disappointmented: this did not feel compassionate to me; but seeing his effect on my son, I accepted his answer, confused but with humility.

It left me thinking for a long time about what he meant: was it more compassion for others, or for myself? But it was astute enough that I am still thinking about it three years later. Janet Croft, a long time friend, likened it to a koan: the mind will work and work on it until it finds the intended result. I realised that I do find it very difficult to have the same compassion for myself that I have for my family or for clients and friends. But I think there has been gradual progress. I am very impressed with how he just repeated the same two words and would not be drawn to say more. It certainly had the effect of making my mind work on it: I simply could not put it down.

AJAHN SUCITTO

I have known Ajahn Sucitto for about twenty-five years, but I had not seen him for many years. Recently I met him again at a three-day core process psychotherapists' conference— On Mindfulness and Beyond—run by the Karuna Institute, at which he was going to give a talk. He asked me how I was doing; I described the nightmare of my cancer experience, and we then parted, as the next lecture was about to commence. After a while, listening to the lecture, I felt something, but was not clear what it was. It made me look up, and there on the far side of the lecture hall was Ajahn Sucitto, looking straight at me. His head at a slight angle, our eyes met but he did not respond. Some time later I felt the need to look up again and there he was, the same look across the hall. It happened about three times during the day: and that look, that sense of his presence, has been with me since. Any time I am worried or anxious, it helps me a great deal and has been tremendously reassuring. It's the knowledge that he is always there when I need him.

Once again, it is the mystery of these spiritual masters' power, that a look can be felt across a crowded lecture hall. The image and sense of his presence is now always with me. All that happened over a period of forty five minutes, and its effect is amazing when you consider the very powerful advertisements on television, that are just forgotten and dismissed. That look of concern and curiosity was so simple and so powerful.

LAMA CHIME

The first time I went to see Lama Chime was at Cambridge. I was immediately struck by his soft warm presence, radiating across his big room. He must have been some ten feet from

me, but he felt very close, his energy holding me in a loving way. He looked at me intently and said, "We've met before." My first reaction was that we definitely had not. The experience was both disconcerting and intriguing, so that, together with his loving and soft presence, it made me just want to laugh. As I did, Chime laughed with me. In a few minutes my troubled mood had gone: everything was alright with the world.

He asked me why I had come, and I told him of my fifteen year history of meditating, from the Maharishi Mahesh Yogi onwards to Bhuddism at Amravati. As I continued, I felt I needed something more encouraging. Then he said, "I've heard a lot about transmission and the Tibetan approach."

"Can it come in dreams?" I asked.

He smiled and told me to stand up while he put his hands one either side of my temples. With his eyes closed, he applied a short firm pressure. I waited, delighted at my luck. But I waited more and absolutely nothing happened. Then, as I was losing hope, a small sensation happened in the right side of my solar plexus. I felt intuitvely that I should let go, but I couldn't. Chime just smiled, and I felt he knew exactly what was going on. He said, "I will give you some meditations. If they work, good; if they do not, don't do them." It was a natural time for me to go, so I thanked him and left.

After that I saw him a couple of times in Cambridge, and once in London at the Dali Lama's talk at the Barbican. He smiled, said hello, and we chatted. Two Taiwanese girls aged about nineteen or twenty approached him and bowed in respect.

"I have to go now for my massage," he told me, with a humorous twinkle in his eyes; and then he was gone.

A couple of years ago I went to a talk in Cambridge. As it ended and the audience dispersed to go home, I was deep in thought. I looked up and found myself walking just behind Chime. I had a sudden intuitive flash that this was the last time I would see him alive. Chime spun around immediately as if I'd spoken aloud, smiled gently, and said quietly, "Time doesn't matter, time doesn't matter, time doesn't matter." He gently tapped his forehead on mine three times. My mind stopped and I was enveloped in a feeling of mystery and awe at how much these Tibetans know that we in the West don't.

30 DAVID

I was expecting a new client. I answered the door to find a tall man about 35 years old with a very intense gaze. He smiled at me and said in a very clipped, 'old colonel' fashion, "Hello. Bernie is it? I'm David."

"Come in, David, make yourself comfortable." He sat in my armchair, surveyed the room and looked at me.

"Now, how do we do this?"

"Well, maybe you could start by telling me what's brought you here."

"A Buddhist ex-client of yours sent me. I am also a Buddhist, and he said you were a psychospiritual psychotherapist who understands Buddhism and Buddhist meditation."

"Yes, that's right; and any questions you want to ask me about your meditation, I'll be happy to answer."

"OK, well, there is something not quite right. I don't know what it is but I'm here to find out." He regarded me challengingly.

"How does this affect you?"

As David started to answer a very interesting thing happened. He put his head down as he searched for the words and moved his head stiffly from side to side as though his neck was hurting him.

"Well, it's uncomfortable… er… a kind of anger, frustration."

His frustration filled the room. He seemed to want it to burst out of him but at the same time didn't know what *it* was.

"Where does this behaviour or feeling manifest itself mostly?"

"Work," came the very swift reply. "Yes, work." And he stopped. This, I soon learned, was the habitual jerky pattern of his sentences.

"David," I encouraged him, "can you say more? There's no rush; and any examples are better for me to get a clearer understanding."

"Right," said David, "examples." He rocked backwards and forwards, looking stern, very 'colonel' like. Then he exploded:

"If I'm doing a job at work it's *my* project—mine. I don't want anybody else interfering, trying to take it from me—it's mine. I get very angry about that. Just leave me alone and let me get on with it my way."

As I sat there listening, perfectly at peace, David suddenly seemed to become aware of how he sounded in the quiet of the room. He looked at me with a stern expression, his head going to one side. Then he softened and continued in quite a different voice, "It's a bit like a kid really, init?" He stopped.

"That's interesting; can you say more?"

"Yeah," responded David, a bit more playfully, "they're my toys and you're not playing with them so how about that?" He looked friendlier and quite pleased with himself.

"Tell me about your childhood."

David paused for a minute.

"Well, I was the first born and there were no complications. My memories are of a happy childhood."

231

He told me he was four when his brother was born.

"Anything else?"

"I had tantrums, was very difficult to handle, and also bullied my brother."

David could look quite fierce, his eyes staring confrontationally at me. Then in a moment his eyes could soften, he would look like a little boy lost and blush slightly.

Somehow any softness, intimacy, has connections in him with shame, I thought. I felt without doubt that he had known great emotional pain in his life and that there was an intense struggle going on in him. His rigidity and staccato sentences reminded me of an old colonel containing himself, keeping himself together.

He was a Buddhist but when he felt strongly his persona could take on that evangelical quality of fire and brimstone.

His voice would often sound like a man wanting so much to appear strong and in control. He was ruthlessly judgmental, but he used this black and white approach predominantly against himself.

I glanced at the clock and David, ever sharp and intense, snapped straight back into regimental mode.

"OK, time's up then is it?" He got up quickly as if he was desperate to do the right thing, gave me a stern look and shook hands.

"Thank you Bernie. See you next week, same time?" And with that he was gone.

A feeling of sadness stayed with me on and off long after our session was over. I kept seeing those sad-stern eyes. They seemed to sum up why he had come, but I wondered what lay behind them...

A TRAGEDY REVEALED

David cocked his head to one side, looking down at me from his six foot frame.

"Good to see you," he said, and stuck out his hand. I liked his manner—he was a character. I wasn't surprised to learn he worked as a salesman.

As David sat down and looked around the room he sighed, breathing very deeply with a hint of the asthmatic. He did in fact have asthma, although interestingly, after four months of therapy, the condition all but vanished. This was not so surprising as asthma often has quite a powerful emotional component to it and giving expression to his repressed emotions quite obviously had an effect on David's particular strain of asthma.

I took out my customary client history form.

"Dave, can you fill this in for me and send it to me, if you can, prior to the next session?" David looked very stern and in his best stiff-upper-lip fashion said, "Yes, yes, I will."

I continued, "You may find that filling in the form will be quite helpful and surprising in what feelings and memories it can bring up in you. That is part of the process of our therapy and a way of giving me your background so that I can get to know what shaped you."

David appeared fascinated and thoughtful. Then he looked at me as though he needed some kind of guidance on how to proceed in our session.

"Just say what you want to say, if there is anything pressing. Otherwise you can carry on explaining about your childhood or any other things you think are important."

David began: "I'm a Buddhist. I was recommended to come to you by another Buddhist who had been in therapy with you so it's nice to find a therapist who understands Buddhism and the practices of Buddhist meditation."

"Good. Any questions you have I will be happy to answer and any meditation problems that come up, we can work with also. It's interesting that you mention your spiritual practice as I am a psychospiritual psychotherapist as opposed to a psychotherapist who deals predominantly with the ego."

David looked serious; then after some thought he said abruptly, "My father was very rigid and controlling."

He stopped, moving his neck about.

"He had a real *thing* about homosexuals." Throwing both hands up in the air he stretched before continuing, "He had very strong mood swings." Pausing again, he moved his neck stiffly before resuming in his jerky fashion, "He would get so frustrated and angry like he was really struggling with something."

I was suddenly struck by the thought that David's demon might be the same as his father's.

"As I got older I became very aware that something was wrong with my dad." David's face clouded over with anxiety and in that moment, I could see the depth of his love for his father.

He stopped, nodded his head vigorously and said, "I've just realised something as I've been speaking. I'm the same as my dad." He looked quite frightened and saddened by this insight.

The overall impression I had was that David's dad was an angry man, who was deeply frustrated about something in his life. He was David's first male role model and had unconsciously conditioned his son to be the same as himself. I felt uncomfortable as if something was looming but I didn't know what.

David went quiet for a while, looking thoughtful. Then he spoke.

"When I was 26 my dad committed suicide." His face looked oddly blank, not registering any emotion.

"David, could you say more about your dad's suicide?"

He replied in a flat, matter of fact tone with hardly any emotion, "He killed himself because he had business problems I suppose."

My sense was that David had not grieved properly and was splitting off from his feelings surrounding his dad's death. Obviously I felt this to be one of the main reasons he had come to therapy.

The session was nearly up and we'd got on to something really crucial. Clients often say something extremely important or difficult for them a few minutes before the end of the session. It's as if it's all they can handle at that moment and unconsciously they know they have some breathing space until the next session.

I felt uncomfortable about looking at the clock and ending the session as it was such a sensitive moment and such an important disclosure. But I picked up the look of relief on David's face as he realised that the session was ending.

"Oh well." David pulled himself together again in regimented fashion, stood up and shot out his hand to shake mine.

"See you next week Bernie."

I found myself left in an emotional limbo with so many unanswered questions. *The poor father*, I thought; *poor David*.

DEFENCE MECHANISM

David sat down looking very uncomfortable. He was quiet for a bit and the atmosphere in the room started to become quite heavy.

"Difficult week, difficult week," he said. Silence.

After a little while I prompted, "What's been difficult, Dave?"

"Been depressed this week, angry too, fed up with the people at work."

"Why? What are they doing?"

Flushed, he spoke very slowly and angrily through gritted teeth.

"They keep interfering with my project!" He seemed physically uncomfortable, moving his neck and his shoulders.

It sent me a message of such powerful energy that I said, "Can you just stay with that movement of your shoulders and neck? You don't have to talk."

He twisted, strained, went red, lifted one shoulder then the other, twisted his neck from side to side, jaw jutting out. He seemed to be struggling to free himself from something holding him. This movement became a regular part of our sessions. Whenever I asked David to exaggerate that movement and stand up without worrying about talking he always experienced considerable emotional relief afterwards.

When David stopped moving he exclaimed, "Ah, that's better," in a way that was nothing like the colonel, but younger and freer. Then right out of the blue he said,

"Yeah, I think he was near a nervous breakdown or had had a nervous breakdown."

"Are you talking about your dad?" I checked.

"Yes," replied David, lapsing into silence once more.

After some time, I prompted, "Could you tell me more about this period?"

"Not really," he replied in an official manner, with an air of disinterest. At this point he went quiet and thoughtful again. I continued to sit calmly to give him the space to think.

It became apparent in this session and following sessions that David had a strong defence mechanism when it came to talking about his father and his father's suicide. He would only say so much, go quite official, then change the subject.

I decided to support his pace of disclosure. So it would pop up in some sessions and then maybe not at all for a good few more. Of course I knew he had to face it, but I felt it was imperative that we build our relationship first.

I heard a train in the distance becoming louder then quieter. David realised we were approaching the end of the session.

"How has the session left you?"

"Well, I still feel angry, but I also feel easier in some way. Amazing, I can't understand that."

"David, it's been quite an intense session, so it may be a good idea to breathe some fresh air and walk slowly to your car before you drive, to give yourself a moment or two."

In that moment David gave me an odd look and replied slowly, as if preoccupied, "OK, I will."

OUT OF CONTROL

David sat reminiscing about leaving school and starting work, prompted by a recent meeting with an old school friend in a firm he had visited in his sales job.

"I had lots of good friends at school and others when I left school, going to pubs and clubs and then…" he frowned… "I think it was around this period that I stopped talking to my parents for a year."

"Why was that?"

"I was just very angry with them but I don't want to talk about that now." *Oh*, I thought, *I wonder why?*

"Later I met my wife to be and after a time we got married." He looked quite sad at this point. "There was something missing." David's face clouded over with unmistakable anxiety.

I wondered whether this was anxiety regarding his marriage. But no. As ever, David surprised me.

"My anger, Bernie, sometimes erupts into road-rage."

I noted this and thought I would come to it later. My mind flashed back to the odd look he gave me at the end of the last session when I asked him to sit in his car for a bit and settle down before driving.

"I take my rage out on my wife—it's like I can't stop myself. I deliberately look for things she does wrong and when she cries I feel guilty." Then he added, "She does get things wrong though."

There was a powerful conflict going on here; and it seemed difficult for him to take responsibility for what he was doing in the marriage. This did not make for a good atmosphere between him and his wife, and I thought David would blame her rather than knowing or owning himself to be the cause.

EXPRESSING DIFFICULT EMOTIONS

In order for David to connect with his feelings and grieve, deal with the shock and impact of his father's suicide and any fears that this terrible event had left him with, I felt he needed to become more aware of his attitude to himself and others. He needed to let go of the terrifically rigid discipline that held him together, and allow much more gentleness into his life.

Excited to find that he was very interested in films, I thought this might be a medium through which he could be helped to express difficult unconscious emotions in order to adjust to them.

I do not usually prescribe movies to my clients, preferring them to bring to me films that have moved them. But in David's case I felt the films *American Beauty* and *Billy Elliot* were relevant examples to use.

In *American Beauty*, Lester Burnham, a depressed suburban father in a mid-life crisis, becomes infatuated with one of his daughter's friends. His daughter, meanwhile, is developing a friendship with the boy next door who lives with a very strict homophobic father, a colonel in the US marines.

In *Billy Elliot*, an 11 year-old boy from a traditional northern mining community, much to his family's consternation rejects the local boxing ring in favour of the girls' ballet class, where the ballet mistress soon realises he has real potential.

In both films there are issues about masculinity and homophobia and, in *American Beauty*, suicide. I was keen to see what the homophobic colonel in *American Beauty* would bring up in David, and whether there was anything he could benefit from in terms of seeing the impact one person could have on their own world.

It was difficult for David to become aware of his spiteful inner critic constantly persecuting him, so I actually showed him the scene where Lester's wife beats herself up by slapping her own face and calling herself a wimp. I wanted to show him what he was doing to himself internally, every hour of every day. The scene helped him to make the link with his depression and its destructiveness in relationships, especially with his wife.

REACTIONS TO *AMERICAN BEAUTY*

As David talked about how *American Beauty* had moved and helped him, I asked him to write down his reactions. I felt this would have the therapeutic value of deepening the experience in him and giving him greater insight and clarity. He agreed, and one day brought a few pages he'd written, which I asked him to read out to me in the session. He wrote:

> "*American Beauty mirrors how much of my life has been spent maintaining a self-image that was false. I was living a lie. I completely identified with Lester in that I too had numbed myself from responsibility, pain and life.*

"My life had become dull, flat, and routine and was very frustrating. It was quite something for me to see in the film how Lester's attitude to life had affected those around him. It became all too clear to me that I had created my own version of that around me. I saw myself in the mirror—flat and dull in mind, body and spirit. I saw most people around me as being flat and dull, even though they weren't. The film showed me that.

"The film stopped me right in my tracks and has left an indelible mark on me. Realising how completely stupid I'd been I started to make amends, so grateful that I still had time to make changes in my life. What if I had died so blinkered? The film gave me much energy to get on with my life, to try and open up, be me, to stop blaming others and to take responsibility.

'I'm writing this some six months after seeing the film. I am still strongly moved and it has left an indelible mark on me."

Here was testimony to the huge and lasting impact of the film on David. Six months later nothing had worn off. He was in fact integrating what he'd got from it. To my amazement he had never even mentioned the colonel. This was a reminder to me that the client is the expert on their own inner feelings and responses.

DOUBTS ABOUT SEXUALITY

David had briefly touched upon some doubts about his own sexuality and in this session he addressed the issue more deeply.

He sat down with a heavy sigh looking very troubled. He rolled his eyes, looked up to the ceiling, sighed again. Finally, he exclaimed, "I don't know Bernie!" I waited, but he said nothing.

"What don't you know Dave?" He glanced at me for a moment, looked away and said, "Me and men. I don't think I am gay but I feel uncomfortable with 'em."

"In what context? Groups? One to one?"

"Oh, one to one—I am fine with groups."

"What's uncomfortable about one to one?"

David now looked embarrassed and blushed. I was impressed with his courage. It's such a sensitive subject, and men with doubts about their sexuality often feel so much shame. Dave continued, "I was in a pub with an old friend Thursday night. It was alright at first but gradually I started to feel self conscious."

"Can you remember what happened just before you had that feeling?" I probed.

"We were enjoying old memories, laughing. We made eye contact I think..." Pause. "Yes, that was it. When I realised we had made eye contact I started to feel uncomfortable."

"Was there any message in the eye contact?"

"No, just innocent enjoyment of the moment."

"How did you feel about him?" Dave looked puzzled, blushed. "Close. I liked him." It was said almost in a whisper as if he was struggling to get the words out.

My inner reaction was that this was just emotional intimacy. I thought I would try something provocative.

"What would your Dad say if he had seen you both?"

David cringed. "Poofs!" he said, almost angrily, blushing to the roots now.

"David," I suggested, "maybe it's emotional intimacy that you are confusing with sexuality?" He was somewhat stunned at this and I decided to work with and talk about the difference between the two. "Intimacy between men or between men and women can lead to sexuality but not necessarily. Intimacy is an important part of healthy male bonding."

Many of the insights David gained from the films were gradually unpacked in the course of our therapy sessions. We would work on vague feelings and sticking points until they became clear or movement became possible. The film *Billy Elliot* helped David deal with his doubts about his sexuality, as he later explained:

"*Billy Elliot* did something to me that literally abated these fears and opened new areas of my character to me, which have given me much comfort. The contrast of the very masculine mining environment to Billy's introduction to ballet dancing showed me that in masculinity, there could be femininity.

"The mixed acceptance of this by Billy's friends and family and his eventual winning through were very powerful for me. In my masculine body I had banned feminine feelings and it suddenly started to feel alright to have them. I could like the colour pink and it was OK. I could enjoy flower arranging, making cakes and do anything that related to the feminine side of me and it was OK. What a release it was--and one that continues to this day."

APPROPRIATE PACE

In my sessions with David I needed to be non-judgemental, gentle and understanding, providing the freedom and space to explore and gently share these taboo subjects and new attitudes. If clients have been brought up in an emotionally, mentally or sexually abusive climate they may deal with their feelings in an abusive way as they have no terms of reference of what a more healthy way would be. Under the illusion that they are working hard in their therapy they may actually end up re-traumatising themselves by recreating and reactivating the trauma they lived through instead of healing it.

Therapists have to be very aware of this and to go at a pace that in their clinical judgement is appropriate and not get sucked in to what may appear to be rapid progress. If the client reports mood swings, flashbacks, sleep disturbance, insomnia and more than usual dreams or nightmares, these are warning signs. Then it is important to slow down so that what's coming up from the unconscious can be integrated at a healthier pace.

Because he had been through a lot, and also for financial reasons, David felt he needed a break from therapy. I considered that the lack of funds was not a mechanism for avoidance, so I looked for a therapeutic way of dealing with the situation. After we discussed this at length we both felt quite comfortable with the arrangement and it was agreed he would come back. I felt the break would help him to integrate the work we had done together so far at his own pace; and if he came up against anything too disturbing he knew he could always ring me.

AN 'UNNAMEABLE' PLACE

In our third session after David's return to therapy I began by asking him what he had noticed over the last week. He thought for a while.

"I noticed that I have the same lack of stability I always connected with my Dad."

"Can you say more about this lack of stability?" Struggling to find words, he took a deep breath.

"It's a kind of mad part."

"Mad part? Is there a predominantly emotional tone to it?"

"Yes, it's like nothing's going to get in its way. It's the part that affects me when I'm driving."

"How?"

He looked sheepish and flushed. "I cut people up."

"You say people, so it's not an isolated incident?"

"No, and I drove someone right off the road once."

"Were they hurt"?

"No. On the pavement though."

He looks worried and puzzled as he acknowledges what he is saying about his behaviour.

"It's like, no one is going to get past me or bully me, but there is something else, it's... it's..." He strains with frustration and then falls into despair. "It's so deep I just can't get to it."

What flashed across my mind was the memory of David saying "no-one is going to take over my project, it's mine". And now we have "no-one is going to overtake me". I just noted it.

"OK, just relax, don't worry, and breathe." Then after this pause I ask, "Can you make a sound from this 'unnameable' place?"

He tried. "No."

"Can you make any physical movement or expression from this place, any shape with your body?"

David slowly started turning his head from side to side. I had a very quick intuitive reaction of what this nodding was and encouraged him to continue. Now his whole body was turning as if he was caught in a web.

"Could you stand up and follow wherever this movement leads?" He stood up, moved, and I saw that the web was a psychosomatic manifestation of his shock and grief at his father's suicide.

"Is there an image or a moment from a film that comes to mind?"

"That's it," he said excitedly. "What comes up is the scene at the beginning of *Saving Private Ryan* where the troops are all under fire on the beach and a man's arm is blown off. It's the way he picked his arm up and looked at it and kind of stomped off like a kid with a toy."

"Like a kind of disorientated shock."

"Yes, that's it." Eyes wide open with a far away look, he seemed young and vulnerable.

The shock on the soldier's face had connected David with his own buried shock over his father's suicide. The scene had allowed him to communicate some madness in himself and to express the unnameable deep feelings. Thus to his great relief he had started to understand the isolated and terrified part of himself, and gradually to free himself from it. It was a transformative moment that I was able to use in our subsequent work together to help him begin the process of healing.

MOMENTS OF REVELATION

In the following session David came in frowning, sat down and looked at me for a while.

"How have you been?" I asked.

"Not bad." He paused. "I had a dream. He paused again and sighed. "Yes, it was a dream of great sadness."

"Great sadness?"

"Yes, sadness that was bottomless."

"What film, if any, could help you with all this?" I was specifically using the term 'all this' to connect with our previous session.

"*A.I.* comes to mind."

A.I. or *Artificial Intelligence* is a film about a highly advanced robotic boy who longs to become 'real' so he can regain the love of his human mother. I asked, "What scene or moment?"

"The blue fairy scene."

"What was it about that scene?"

"Well," David sighed, "all that happened to him with his family—I identified with that." Then looking distant and lost he added, "It was the time he waited for an answer."

David went deeply into himself for a while. I noticed the atmosphere in the room. It had that special quietness that can come at important moments of insight, of revelation. His face brightened.

"Hope," he said strongly, clearly, "it represented hope to me."

"Anything else?" I asked slowly, quietly.

"Space," he said softly. Then after a period of quiet he said, "That one day stays with me—it keeps coming back to me."

In the film the boy is granted a wish that he can have one day with his mum. She is brought back to life as he remembers her. His experience of having lost her and his knowledge that this day with her will end only fuels his intensity and appreciation of her all the more.

"How would you like to spend your one day?"

"With my dad."

His choice might have seemed a surprising, given how David had experienced his dad as rigid and controlling, with many frightening mood swings. But this was in retrospect, with David's dad having been dead for some time, and David knowing the shocking manner in which he had died. Also, the fact that David had been in therapy and had got to know himself much better had, in many senses, given him a deeper understanding of his dad.

"What would you say to him?"

The look of great sadness came across David's face.

"Dad, I love you. But it's more that I would just want to be with him, with no demands." His eyes suddenly brightened. "Funny, my mum got me a card with a picture of a man and a boy on a boat looking out to sea—that just came up."

"So is that how you would like to spend the day with your dad?"

"Yes, yes, I would."

"What I notice is your need for space, no demands, for hope and time to be with what's important to you. This is what you seem to take from the film."

"Oh yes, thank you," he said, "this has been like a breath of fresh air to me."

His response came as something of a surprise, for I was unaware of quite how deeply the scene from the film and our analysis of his fantasy had affected him.

"I wonder if it's possible for you to take some space free of any demands this weekend on your own?"

David looked shocked as though my simple question had somehow jolted him out of his habitual rigidity of focus. Then his expression changed to one of excitement and he smiled broadly.

"Why not?" I said.

"Yes, why not indeed? I'll do it this weekend in a town or village near me somewhere."

In this session David had been able to find a scene from a film to nurture him and show him what he needed. He was then able to act on it by planning to take some space in order to find hope and to begin to heal.

COINCIDENCES?

When David came in I was quite struck by the quality of energy about him. There was something lighter, something different, and I told him so.

He looked up at me with a sort of boyish smile.

"Yes, Bernie, I really feel different." Placing his hands on both knees he went on, "Well, I did it! I started to talk to my mum about the things I didn't know, about their relationship and about possible reasons why my dad had committed suicide. I know that for the last 15 years I've been very angry with her.

"I took her paper up, as she was staying over the weekend at my place, and I sat on the edge of the bed and started to ask her. At first she said it was all a very long time ago and that we should forget it; but I persisted. I reminded her that she and my brother had been living with my dad and must have had some ideas of the build-up to his taking his own life. I on the other hand had just received a phone call to say that he was dead."

David said his mum was in tears. She told him that his dad had got obsessed with building his business and just wouldn't include her. There were things he was doing that she couldn't go along with and she had told him so.

Then David asked when her man friend had come on the scene. His mum looked guilty and explained how worried she had been when his father had completely refused to communicate with her. She had desperately needed someone to talk to. David asked, "Did Dad know?" His mum said she didn't think so because the man was a family friend.

David looked at me and said, "This is all helping so much: pieces of the puzzle are beginning to fit together inside me."

"Do you feel your mum told you everything?"

He looked me in the eye.

"No, not at all. She was very wary and very careful in what she said."

"So you've made a great beginning in what appears to be an ongoing conversation?"

"Yes, and I do need to know the rest of it."

I agreed that he did, otherwise he could speculate for another 15 years.

"Only when these repressed feelings and secrets are out in the open is there the possibility that you, your mum and your brother will be able to grieve fully and have a real relationship."

David looked at me and nodded.

I mentioned that, watching the news over the weekend, I had been astounded by the strange coincidence of the death of Dr David Kelly—the government scientist who, like David's father, had committed suicide by taking sleeping tablets and slashing his wrists in a lonely field. David nodded very quickly.

"Strange, certainly. The reports were everywhere—on the radio, TV and in the newspapers."

"The timing is uncanny."

"Yes, yes," David nodded vigorously then paused. "It's like when my mum was stopped by a market research lady in town."

"I haven't heard about that."

"Well," he said, "my mum said she was in too much of a hurry to spend time filling in her form but the lady insisted she had something to tell her. She explained she was a medium and shocked my mum by saying she knew that her husband was dead. When my mum confirmed in a whisper that this was the case the woman said my dad was there with her, with a message asking why my mum hadn't found someone and remarried, and why she wasn't getting on with her life? Shocked and crying, my mum thanked the woman, who apologised saying she just had to pass these things on."

Just as David finished telling me this story a pigeon flew on to the window sill. The window was wide open and it appeared that the pigeon was gong to come into the room. It just stood on the window sill looking straight at David who looked directly back, smiling slightly, his face red and full of emotion and with tears in his eyes. The atmosphere in the room changed. It was a quiet sacred moment, as if something really unusual was happening on another level of consciousness. When with a flap of the wings the pigeon flew away, David looked at me and sighed, "Wow."

I believed I knew exactly what had just happened, but I thought I'd ask David just one question and then give him space to stay in the moment with something very powerful going on inside him.

"You looked very moved by that David. What happened there?"

David looked at me, more relaxed than I had ever seen him, and said smiling softly, "It's my dad. That was like a message, the pigeon. I have such an experience of presence in the room now, can you feel it?"

"Yes, I can. You just stay with the experience and I'll keep quiet."

David sat there in silence, smiling, tears coming into his eyes, occasionally sighing, for about ten minutes. Then he said, "Boy! I've never had an experience like this. I just feel so looked after—like the universe is holding me. It's like that scene in *American Beauty* where the Lesters' young neighbour is fascinated to see a carrier bag being played with by the wind. You get the sense of something behind everything."

He then reviewed everything that had happened—the fact that his mother had come the last weekend, his decision for the first time in fifteen years to confront her with the questions, then his mum's experience with the medium in the street and finally the uncanny experience with the pigeon. The next surprise was when he told me it had also been his dad's birthday last Saturday. He said, "It feels like a process of things all working together, all falling in place."

Time was moving on now and David seemed to know this unconsciously. He gave me a very heartfelt look. "Thank you Bernie, thank you for being there."

I just replied with the sense of humility I felt.

"Thank you for sharing all this with me, and for this moment. Our work has been not just psychological, but psychospiritual. I must say I have never experienced anything quite like what just happened in all my years as a therapist."

David smiled, got up, looked so relaxed and shook my hand vigorously.

"Bye, Bernie, see you next week."

"I look forward to it."

I walked back into my session room. The room was very quiet and the sense of what had just happened was echoing inside me. I sat down, quite tired, gazing out of the open window from my chair and feeling the warm wind come in. *That,* I thought, *was incredible.* Until you have an encounter like that it can be difficult to believe. There are many forces we don't know much about in this life.

MISSING PIECES OF THE JIGSAW

David came today. He had a kind of tentative manner that was unusual for him.

"Well, er, nice to see you."

"Yes, and you," I replied smiling.

He looked down at the Tesco bag he had brought with him, glanced back at me, then said, "OK, I might as well…"

stopping mid sentence. He reached for the bag and pulled out an old telephone directory with some handwriting on the back in green ball point pen.

"That's it," said David sliding it towards me. There was a real sense of him trying to hold himself together.

I picked up the directory and saw it was David's father's suicide note. I read it realising this was a very significant moment. These were the last words that David's dad had felt compelled to write as he lay dying—just about ten sentences.

As I felt the book in my hands I was in the field where his dad was found. *A strange choice to write a suicide note on a telephone directory in green ink.*

David was looking at me. He looked young now, vulnerable and restless.

"I don't know where to put myself," he said nervously, half smiling.

"No," I said, "just let yourself go with this very important moment. This is really why you came to therapy—unresolved grief and shock. You've carried the burden of all this for fifteen years and it has greatly affected your life. You've put up a superhuman struggle of the stiff upper lip kind and so has your family. This is the reason none of you can connect. Nurture one another, cry, speak heart to heart. That is what you are all so yearning for."

David's eyes filled with tears and he nodded vigorously.

"You are so right, so right. We try over and over again but it never works." His voice cracks a bit. "No, how could it? It's all unresolved and you bounce off one another's defences. You know," he went on, "as you speak it's all falling into place, like missing pieces of the jigsaw."

THE BEAUTIFUL BOY

David came in very stern and stiff upper lipped and said, "Hello, how are you?"

"Fine," I answered.

"Good, good," said David sounding more and more like a colonel.

I said, "Let yourself arrive after the long journey you have had in traffic, and just see what comes to you without any trying."

"Yes, yes," said David in his clipped fashion, starting to take his shoes off. It was a very warm day so I opened the session room window. A police car siren whizzed by which irritated me. David looked more relaxed and miles away. Then he said, "When I was young I used to wake up bright as a button, but I used to go to sleep angry. I wanted to wake up angry to show 'em."

"Show who?" I asked.

"My mum and dad, but mainly my dad."

"How did you do that?" David thought for a while. "I just closed down my beautiful boy's feelings and got more involved with anger."

I immediately made the connection with John Lennon's song 'Beautiful Boy' to his own son. I mentioned this to David, because I felt intuitively that the song's complete contrast with his own experience could be turned into support for him whenever he chose to listen to it.

"You kind of killed that part of your self? It feels like you experienced such disillusionment, such disappointment."

"Yes, it was like that."

"What was the *it*?"

"They didn't see that fresh, bright, sensitive part of me—my beauty."

"How old were you? Why did you do it?"

"Six, seven, eight maybe. To think I did all that to align myself with my dad's anger because his anger frightened and worried me."

It is important to understand that David's dad was quite volatile. His anger and his unpredictability terrified David and created a tension-filled atmosphere. David's first response was to withdraw from the family by not talking. There was more than one reason for this. First he was keeping out of the way because it felt safer, but he was also inadvertently punishing his parents who tried hard to get him to talk. The other spin-off was that he was getting attention, but not the kind he needed. Then he began to adopt a different tactic: aligning himself with his dad's moods and anger, as a way to deflect conflict with his father.

Unfortunately he took his learned adaptive self into his life in general and all his relationships; which made things difficult—for example, in the relentless picking on his wife when he was angry. When he had told me this I had been so reminded of his dad. He was unconsciously recreating the very atmosphere he had so hated at home.

"How did it affect you when your dad committed suicide?"

"I was shaken, but I had learned to suppress my feelings—so well, in fact, that now I can't do otherwise."

I was interested in his short 'I was shaken' answer, and then the way he fell back on being angry and rigid. This was his dad's legacy, a destructive pattern that had led to suicide.

I was trying to decide how I could help him to free himself from this anger, this rigidity.

"David, we've got to this depth, this mood in the session. Is there any film that comes to mind?"

After thinking for a moment David replied, "Yes, *The Matrix*."

"What was it that you identified with?"

"Things are not what they seem."

Inside I wondered *What things? How is this connected to his dad? Does he mean his dad was not what he seemed?*

SUB-PERSONALITIES

We all have what can be termed sub-personalities: different characteristics that are unconscious and often in conflict with one another. In our sessions it had become clear that David was wrestling with two conflicting sub-personalities. His number one sub-personality, his pacifying part, kept his feelings buttoned up. It was the response he had developed to deal with his father's unpredictability and his fear of becoming like him. This pacifying part was constantly saying things to him like "It's OK"; "It will be alright"; "Forget about it"; "You worry too much, let me deal with it"; and "You mustn't say that".

David's other sub-personality, his rage part, was the product of his unexpressed grief and shock at his father's death. It revealed itself in sudden eruptions of anger.

I asked David to act out what he wanted the one sub-personality to say to the other. What did his rage part want to say to his pacifying part?

He spat out, "I want to be listened to!" His voice rose to a shout. "I don't want to be humoured, I don't want to be pacified." And again, "I want to be listened to; can you just listen!"

I say, "Now, please, with all your feeling, tell your pacifying part how this being humoured and not listened to has affected you."

Once again David's rage part answered. His face was bright red as he pounded the cushions, making the room shake with the vibration. He shouted, "Just listen to me. Just don't ignore me. Just acknowledge me. See me. It's like I don't exist. It's like in some nice way you are always telling me to shut up. I have a contribution and I have a point of view and I want a life!"

The sweat was dripping off David's forehead onto the cushion. The room was incredibly hot.

When I asked David's pacifying part to respond it looked dumbstruck, saying in almost a whisper, "I feel so guilty." Pause. "I never realised your pain."

David looked up again, made direct eye contact and said quietly, "This moment, Bernie, will change my life forever."

HEALING

I had asked David to bring to this session other aspects of *American Beauty* that had been meaningful for him.

"What scene moved you?"

"When she fell into the wardrobe. Too late she realises she loves him." He remembered the part where there is a Kevin Spacey voice-over saying, '*I look back on every moment of my life with absolute gratitude*'.

"I feel that."

I asked gently, "Can you remember any other time when you felt that?" Pause.

"Yeah, walking in the country through the arch of poplar trees outside our village, holding my mum's hand."

"Was that before the beautiful boy in you was crushed?"

He looked at me like a little boy, tears falling slowly down his cheeks.

"Yes, I suppose it was."

"How old were you?"

"Six," he said almost straight away.

"So now you're holding her hand again after all these years?"

The beauty of observing and sharing this moment with David was indescribable. He looked at me and said in a simple, heartfelt way, "Thank you Bernie. Thank you so much."

AFTERWORD

Recently at a friend's house I was recalling a fascinating psychic experience that happened in a session with my client David, as described in the final chapter of this book.

We were discussing his father's suicide when suddenly a pigeon flew onto the sill of the open window. As it looked intently at David the whole atmosphere of the room changed and became very still. My client's face flushed a healthy glow as he smiled a smile of deep inner contentment, tears overflowing.

The room's atmosphere could now only be described as sacred. The pigeon then flew away. David sat there for a bit looking stunned before looking across at me.

"Phew! Did you feel what happened there?"

"Yes," I said, "but what did you feel?"

"That the pigeon was a message from my dad," he replied. It was a deeply healing experience for David and for me.

Because David had agreed that the case study of his therapy could be included in my book I was able to mention this unusual incident to my friend who is a Freudian psychoanalytic psychotherapist. My friend chortled "Rubbish!" He thought it was hilarious.

It made me reflect once again that Freudian psycho-analysis is about understanding and knowing, whereas the Jungian experience of mystery goes beyond the limits of Freud's conceptual knowing. Jungian thought, like Buddhism, embraces the deep regions of healing mystery, whose meaning and influence permeate the very fabric of our soul at the level beyond words and thought.

From the point of view of Buddhism, a film can be described as an orchestration of energies bringing together the story, the actors' talents and particular qualities, the music, the sound, and the director's energy and sensitivity, combined with that of the cameraman. The way the film is shot, with lights, colour and visual impact, and with the director as the conductor, means that certain members of the audience will be the receivers of a vibration of energy on the necessary energetic alignment—hence a transmission.

Therapy can help to integrate, understand, assist and support that healing transmission.

Bernie Wooder, June 2011

www.ingramcontent.com/pod-product-compliance
Lightning Source LLC
Chambersburg PA
CBHW072116270326
41931CB00010B/1578

* 9 780956 075116 *